CW00734836

Precious and Impossible:
Selected Poems

By the same author

Poetry

Sonnets for Albert
Rubber Orchestras
Bird Head Son
Teragaton
Desafinado

Fiction

The Frequency of Magic
Kitch: A Fictional Biography of a Calypso Icon
The African Origins of UFOs

Albums

The Rich Are Only Defeated When Running For Their Lives
People of The Sun
Caribbean Roots
Time
Live in Bremen
Rubber Orchestras
Bird Head Son
Leggo de Lion

Precious and Impossible: Selected Poems

ANTHONY JOSEPH

With an introduction by
Professor Lauri Scheyer

BLOOMSBURY POETRY
LONDON · OXFORD · NEW YORK · NEW DELHI · SYDNEY

BLOOMSBURY POETRY
Bloomsbury Publishing Plc
50 Bedford Square, London, WC1B 3DP, UK
29 Earlsfort Terrace, Dublin 2, Ireland

BLOOMSBURY, BLOOMSBURY POETRY and the Diana logo
are trademarks of Bloomsbury Publishing Plc

First published in Great Britain 2024

Copyright © Anthony Joseph, 1994, 1997, 2009, 2011, 2022, 2024

Introduction copyright © Lauri Scheyer

Anthony Joseph has asserted his right under the Copyright, Designs and
Patents Act, 1988, to be identified as Author of this work

All rights reserved. No part of this publication may be reproduced or
transmitted in any form or by any means, electronic or mechanical,
including photocopying, recording, or any information storage
or retrieval system, without prior permission in writing
from the publishers

A catalogue record for this book is available from the British Library

ISBN: PB: 978-1-5266-5121-1; eBook: 978-1-5266-5119-8;
ePDF: 978-1-5266-5118-1

2 4 6 8 10 9 7 5 3 1

Typeset by Laura Jones-Rivera
Printed and bound in Great Britain by
CPI Group (UK) Ltd, Croydon CR0 4YY

To find out more about our authors and books
visit www.bloomsbury.com and sign up for our newsletters

For Louise

Contents

A Critical Perspective   xi

Desafinado

islands   1

the art of ageing   2

clark boots   5

time slipped   6

constipated irises   7

play in the sunshine   9

west ken' winter   10

angels wearin' tens   12

trees   13

monsters   14

from a tie dyed vase   16

saturday   17

70   18

tobago   19

Teragaton

blakdadamasonsong   25

europeisinmyass   26

camel, a small painting   32

tincture   33

the buff   34

a guava tree   35

indian red   38

garden   39

tigerbalm   40

black&white dark shadows   42

wildlife   43

ting   45

asafoetida   49

coffee   57

carbide   63

9   68

The Jazz Crusaders Live in *New York*   69

Bird Head Son

Conductors of his Mystery   75

Bosch's Vision   78

Punk   80

Sylvia   81

Sophocles   82

Bermudez   83

The Carnival Suite   84

Blockorama   88

Bird Head Son   90

The Tropic of Cancer   93

Mr Buller   95

Bougainvillea: Super 8 Red   97

Blues for Cousin Alvin   108

Jack Spaniard nest   110

Curtis   112

Cutlass   114
Santa Cruz   117
The Bamboo Saxophone   118
Carenage   120
The Regal   122

Rubber Orchestras

Heritage   127
Dimanche Gras   129
Sonnet   131
Rhinoceri   132
Red Dragon Band   133
Présence Africaine   134
Speak the Name   135
Capybara   137
To Paint is to Wound   139
Blue Hues   140
In Baptist Distances   143
Fire Music   144
Two Inch Limbo   145
Griot   146
The Reverend   148
Haiti   149
Woodbrook   151
Philly's Congo Prayer   152
Poem for Franklin Rosemont   154
Angela   156
Audrey   157
Nations   158

A Ditch of Knives   159
Lester Young   160
Riff For Morton   161
In Vibrant Oases   163

Sonnets for Albert

light   167
flack and hathaway   168
jogie road   169
axe   171
what do i know of my father's body?   172
rings   173
el socorro   175
tina   176
breakfast in dc   177
the tumuli in santa cruz   179

Uncollected Poems

Jabbie, the Tailor   185
Manifesto II   188
Dubwise   189
Four Shovels   191
Written from Memory   193
The Inconsolable   195
The Kora   197
Aunt Pat, Bené and the Hurricane   201
In Istanbul   205
Comets   206

Selected Lyrics

Robberman	215
Time: Archeology	217
Girl with a Grenade	220
Heir (For Woman Who Wish)	222
Shine	224
Kezi	226
Suffering (This Savage Work)	229
On the Move	231
Calling England Home	235
Language	237
Smallholding: Eclogue	240
Drum Song	242
Brother Davis (Yanvalou)	246
Caribbean Roots	247
Cobra	250

A Critical Perspective
by Professor Lauri Scheyer

It's been a long journey for Anthony Joseph across the thirty years (1994–2024) of poems collected in this landmark volume. In the 1990s, Joseph was often described as 'the leader of the black avant-garde in Britain' based on his experimental chapbook *Desafinado* (1994) and *Teragaton* (1997). He was stylistically associated with other Black diasporic poets who were equally resistant to following the mainstream, such as Kamau Brathwaite, Ted Joans, Amiri Baraka and Aimé Césaire. Joseph's first two books were self-published by poisonenginepress, which he started as a collective enterprise to feature innovative poetry that was often overlooked in the cultural and literary climate of the 1990s.[1]

As a specialist in avant-garde poetry of the Black diaspora, I was introduced to Joseph at the start of the millennium by our mutual friend Vanessa Richards, who knew I would be fascinated by his work. After reading the two books he had then published, I was mesmerised by his self-possessed voice which drew on multiple traditions with great originality. In 2004, I was invited to direct a pilot British Council Writer-in-Residence programme that would enable a British poet to spend one month at California State University in Los Angeles. There were innumerable wonderful poets to potentially invite. Although he was not well known at the time, the only name I put forward to be the inaugural poet for this programme was Anthony Joseph, who delivered a residency that participants still discuss today. Even then, it was clear to all who encountered his work that this was an exceptional poet with a remarkable future.[2]

Fast-forward three decades: Joseph has a PhD in Creative Writing from Goldsmiths, an academic career, multiple poetry collections and novels to his name, and fronts an internationally respected band as its lead singer and songwriter. Joseph's fifth poetry collection, *Sonnets for Albert* (2022) – composed in an iconic form of the English poetry tradition – was published by Bloomsbury Poetry, a literary press, and won the T. S. Eliot Prize and the OCM BOCAS Prize for Poetry in 2023, the same year he was elected a Fellow of the Royal Society of Literature. What transformation – if any – occurred in those three decades that has led to lionising a poet previously seen as an outsider and renegade?

As a starting point, it's essential to recognise the role of Joseph's family and his origins in Trinidad. Born in Port of Spain on 12 November 1966, Joseph was a 'carnival baby' and the first-born child to young newlyweds Janet (née Guevara) and Albert Joseph. A second child, Dennis, was born to the couple in 1968. Joseph was two years old and Dennis an infant when Janet and Albert divorced. Joseph went to live with his paternal grandmother Sylvia Albertina Lezama (to whom his first poetry collection, *Desafinado*, is dedicated) and step-grandfather Clarence Hoyte in Mt. Lambert, a middle-class suburb that was Albert's hometown. Dennis resided with their mother, who went on to have four more children, while Albert had an additional eight, who comprise Joseph's large circle of half-siblings. His contact with both parents was minimal in his early years which intensified the impact of his attachment to them and their influence. Joseph's poetry often combines auto-biography with fragmentation and surrealism in a reflection of these fractured core connections that runs parallel to his relationship with Trinidad and the Caribbean experience.

Of his five poetry books, the covers of three are family photos, and family photos appear internally in all but one, his fourth collection, *Rubber Orchestras* (2011). A 1970 photo of Anthony and Dennis accompanies the poem 'the art of ageing (for Dennis)' in his first poetry book, *Desafinado*.[3] The cover of his second book, *Teragaton*, is a wedding photo of his parents; Janet was pregnant with Anthony, making it a photo of the poet even before his birth. A childhood photo of Anthony and Dennis appears on the cover of his third collection, *Bird Head Son* (2009). Numerous photos of Joseph's father appear in his fifth collection, *Sonnets for Albert* (2022), whose cover, symbolically, is a photo of Albert looking away with his back to the camera.

From the time of Joseph's childhood, writing poetry and exposure to both esteemed and folk art held an important place in weaving together the disparate strands of his world. A marvellous teller of folktales and invented stories, his grandmother Sylvia often spoke a French Creole patois which struck Joseph as a magical secret language that combined in his developing imagination with bits of Hindi that he overheard from local Indian farmers and the English mainly spoken at home and school. At age eight, Joseph began to accompany his grandparents to the Spiritual Baptist Church in Brazil, Trinidad. During these four-hour services, he encountered glossolalia and the preaching oratory, which added yet another layer to the rich cultural and linguistic magic and fragmentation of his childhood. While Albert was largely absent from Joseph's life, his role was profound and suffuses the poetry. It is not inconsequential that Albert later became a Baptist minister who was known for his oratorical gifts. Although never religious himself, the trappings of his childhood exposure to Black Baptist worship made a lasting impression on Joseph. According to him, 'The Baptist church was the most powerfully magical thing I experienced as a child.'[4] The church services combined the profane and sacred in a multi-sensory encounter with fear, excitement, danger and arousal. This gumbo generated a sense of transcending the mundane that has continued to inspire his poetry and performances.

Joseph describes his childhood best friends as his radio and his notebook. At age twelve, Joseph started filling his notebook with original lyrics to pop songs and these 'song poems' evolved over time into poetry. From his youth, he was surrounded by an eclectic assortment of music which has remained a constant creative force as seen in the incorporation of his song lyrics in *Precious and Impossible*. At home and with friends, he listened to the era's popular rock music (Black Sabbath, Frank Zappa, Led Zeppelin), jazz (Ornette Coleman, John Coltrane), reggae, calypso and carnival music. His household had few books and no bookcase as his grandparents' literary interests were confined to the Bible. They had a record collection which included the famed calypsonian, The Mighty Sparrow, whose double-entendres mesmerised Joseph by showing language's potential to be unstable and have unfixed and multiple meanings.

In 1989, when Joseph left Trinidad for the first time to travel to London, he knew he could never fully return to the country of his childhood and memory, which is the crucial hinge between autobiography and surrealism in Joseph's poetry. In *Black, Brown & Beige: Surrealist Writings from Africa and the Diaspora*, an anthology where Joseph's work appears, co-editors Franklin Rosemont and Robin D. G. Kelley claim that surrealism is not a break from realism but a truer and deeper realism that reveals what is hidden. That definition is helpful to understand how surrealism and realism operate in Joseph's poetry. As he speculates, 'It was almost as if in my dislocation from home and culture, I was trying to find within the text, or at least to record my memory of Trinidad. At this point the whole modus of my writing seemed to congeal into surrealism … going to the Baptist church with my grandparents, seeing the spirit possessions and hearing the glossolalia ... breaking language into morsels of liquid text – all these informed the surreal for me' (Rosemont and Kelley, 337). In inheriting the English language from a colonising culture, which is already not natural, Joseph's poetry is nostalgic for a ' pre-language' that can only be imagined; an impossible effort to recreate or retain which also applies to memories of his homeland.

At the time he was writing the poems in *Desafinado*, Joseph was listening to bossa nova, samba and other Brazilian music. The Portuguese word 'desafinado' is translated as 'off key' or 'out òf tune' and alludes to Antonio Carlos Jobim's song by that name. In the 1990s, some readers of his early poetry found it strange, which he decided to embrace in the title of his first book. Joseph asked his artist friend, Adrian Owusu, to create the stylised drawings (gratis – 'I had no money') that illustrate the book. These images, which capture the psychedelic atmosphere of the era, are preserved in the present volume, creating a sense of living history. For Joseph, sound, image and language have always been inextricable.

The poems selected from his first book highlight Joseph's early poetic experiments with style and perspective, including 'islands' and 'tobago', which locate the origins and trajectory of Joseph's poetry in the Caribbean, the creative anchor which is often personified. The distaff of these island poems appears in the poem 'west ken' winter', depicting the transition from life in the greenery of Mt. Lambert to the reduced space of a dingy 18 x 12 room. The role of family is already pronounced in Joseph's first book: 'the art of ageing' was written on the occasion of Dennis becoming a father; the idolisation of Albert's magical power and magnetism is described in 'Clark Boots'; Janet and Sylvia poignantly meld in the poem 'Trees' whose dedication is 'for my mothers'. Music is an omnipresent theme starting in

Joseph's first book, as shown in such poems as 'from a tie dyed vase' and 'Saturday' (with the dedication 'for zedd', his band at the time).

The relatively clipped lines and legible narratives of *Desafinado* radically shift three years later in *Teragaton*. The title of *Teragaton* came from a dream after his mother's death where she appeared to him and spoke this mysterious word, and it is here we encounter the style that Joseph has referred to as 'liquid textology'. This state evokes the early lessons that he gained from the church services which freed language from pre-determined semantics and syntax and re-engaged the body in the creative act. For Joseph, 'Teragaton' represents a place where the poet departs from the sequences of sense and logics of language to arrive in an unconscious or preconscious state of surrealism and automatic writing. The goal of accessing this space is to resist what Joseph considers to be re-colonisation by means of conceptual control. Its other purpose is to awaken audiences from passively absorbing the text in order to become participants in the act of sense-remaking. The surrealism and avant-garde character of Joseph's writing become legible when seen in this light of recreating a poetics of independent thinking, in order to re-access a truer realism. In 'blakdadamasonsong', Joseph essentially creates his own 'blaksurrealistmanifesto' and his '*OBEAH MANTRAS*' which evoke the historical avant-garde movements and their manifestos (futurism, surrealism, Dada) that also opened his creative horizons. He utilises the examples of these movements as a mode of resistance to the control of mainstream power structures. This overcoming of restrictive cultural boundaries is shown quintessentially in 'europeisinmyass' where all the words are run together in a six-page block of text which re-integrates the visual and verbal aspects of language with their semantic sense. In Joseph's words, this process is an exploration of ways to reconstitute wholeness: 'The text represents a hyperspacial discourse in which Euromericafricarribean agents all have offices in the belly of this beast'.[5]

The theme of family is still evident and preserved in 'the buff', which is dedicated to Albert, and 'a guava tree', an especially beautiful elegy for Janet who died tragically young at the age of 47, in the same year that *Teragaton* was published. 'black&white dark shadows' recollects the intimate and scary experience of watching the eponymous television show with his grandmother. The section of *Teragaton* titled 'teragatonic sampling', which mirrors the process of seizing and repositioning sound references from one piece of music to another, is described by Joseph as 'a Collage of notes, quotes, found text, dialogue', reinforcing the importance of music, the relationship between sound and language, and the influence of popular culture and its visual imagery.

Bird Head Son underscores the prominent place in Joseph's life of his distant father, as seen in his earliest poetry and coming to a crescendo in *Sonnets for Albert*. 'Bird Head' was one of Albert's nicknames, given to him because of his physical appearance. *Bird Head Son* may be viewed in some respects as an artist's draft or preliminary study for *Sonnets for Albert*. This third collection signifies masterful progression by integrating the avant-garde explorations of the earlier volumes with confident control over canonical English forms and styles. Joseph increasingly interweaves what Brathwaite called the 'nation language' of Caribbean oral and vernacular diction and rhythms with that of contemporary English poetry to seamlessly form its own natural world – the poet's world. The effect on readers is to imitate the sensation of living in multiple worlds, times and places. If we attend to the development and cues of his oeuvre, Joseph provides us with a clear map to follow the themes and goals of his poetry that might – especially in the early volumes – have seemed strange or daunting. Read closely, this poetry is the essence of lucidity without compromising its original and individualistic methods and intents. The title poem 'Bird Head Son', dedicated to Brathwaite, correlates the importance of Joseph's biological father with a literary father in the older poet. In subtle but quick cuts, the poem floats between delicate post-Romantic imagery and the vernacular of persona poetry and speech in action. For example, the last stanza of section 1 reads: 'The leaping tongues of flame / that plead with the darkness to wait / Night is a secret a promise to keep / What burns / in the black peppers soot / of leaf and feather / when he fans the flame.' The poem immediately shifts into spoken language located in the past, in Trinidad, at the start of section 2: 'An dat guava tree root dat burn too'. The instability of time and culture even vacillates within sections as the poet rejects the sufficiency of only one language, one time and one world to depict reality. The beauty of the final quatrain of this poem is among the most touching of all of Joseph's poems: '"Ai, you is bird head son? / You mus be bird head son f'true / cause your father head / did small too."' Once again, this volume extends and amplifies the central themes of Joseph's poetry as seen in his earliest publications: language as an exploratory medium, family relationships, music from multiple traditions, the lingering and very real existence of the past in the present and future, and the representation of life as a cacophony instead of a singular story. Or a story comprised of multitudes of perspectives and voices.

Rubber Orchestras pays homage to a quotation from African American surrealist poet Ted Joans: 'I poem my life to poetry …

I visit rubber orchestras'. In this phrase, a favourite of Joseph's, Joans denies that there is a separation between life and poetry, and both are endlessly malleable performances, which has been a guiding principle for Joseph's poetic practice. The poem 'Nations' opens with an epigraph from Gaston Bachelard's *The Poetics of Space*, 'Poetry dominates meaning', and in this collection, poetry has firmly gained control and precedence over non-aesthetic narratives. Selections from *Rubber Orchestras* also include 'Poem for Franklin Rosemont', whose career was devoted to exploring surrealism and especially the margins and furthest reaches of this style, including Black diasporic surrealism. Music is omnipresent in all three sections of his fourth poetry book but is the primary theme of the second section which name-checks the great practitioners of blues, jazz, calypso, Caribbean swing, African instrumentation, and the rhythms and melodies of the cosmos. This volume feels like a wild chorus and in fact it coordinates with an LP by the same name released simultaneously. *Rubber Orchestras* is more fully international in its scope than the preceding volumes and more explicitly oriented towards global musics, as we see in 'Riff For Morton', 'Lester Young', 'In Vibrant Oases', 'Philly's Congo Prayer' and others. There may not be any family photos in *Rubber Orchestras*, but the poems create their own rich linguistic montages of Port of Spain, Harlem, European capitals, the Caribbean, carnival, jazz musicians and touchstones of the African diaspora. Here the original thematics persist: this volume connects to the focus on family, especially Albert, as found in the previous books and serves as precursor to the book which will come next through the poem titled 'Sonnet', which is about Albert.

Sonnets for Albert has been extensively reviewed and often described as 'luminous', radiating light on the simultaneous presence and absence of Albert in life and death. He died in 1997, yet was both a distant spirit and a guiding light while still alive. Robert Hayden's 'Those Winter Sundays' comes to mind as a comparable unconventional sonnet in its conveyance of the complex emotion that a son feels towards his father. With a few exceptions (notably, 'Tina'), the diction of these sonnets is closer to Baptist liturgy than vernacular. The poem 'Axe' combines both. Photos of Albert as a young and old man add poignance to poems whose points of view shift from the poet in youth and maturity who comes to a peaceful resolution with this complex relationship. A key to the indelible impact of the absent father appears as the closing couplet of 'Breakfast in DC' in describing a meal during a literary conference: 'And what we shared, besides our blackness, / was that in our childhoods, our fathers had all been absent'.

In many respects, *Sonnets for Albert* was a long time in the making. Early sonnets for Albert appear even amid Joseph's most experimental poems. *Sonnets for Albert* may be viewed as Joseph's cross-over volume in its use of the familiar form of the contemporary sonnet (eschewing such features as the Shakespearean rhyme scheme and iambic pentameter) and its explicitly articulated focus on the poet's elegiac accounting of his paternal relationship. Through its honours and awards, it earned a wider readership than his earliest books and gained recognition for Joseph as a poet who could address a large and varied audience. Yet *Precious and Impossible* invites readers to look back at his prior five poetry books to discover or rediscover many magnificent poems and follow Joseph's path to this deservedly acclaimed book.

The phrase 'Precious and Impossible' is the title of the second section of Joseph's book *Rubber Orchestras* (2011). The phrase appears again in a previously unpublished poem in the present book, 'The Inconsolable', which is dedicated to his dear friend, the writer Kemal Mulbocus, who tragically died in a car accident at age 39 in 2007. The uncollected poems in *Precious and Impossible*, some of which Joseph worked on for years, include some of the most remarkable works in this volume. The exquisite title poem is deeply personal and important to Joseph. Decontextualised, it might be easy to misunderstand the meaning of this book's title phrase. In context, 'The Inconsolable' is an elegy to a friend who died far too young. This poem juxtaposes past and present in an omen of the broken promises of the future: 'It was summer / and you said that dying was fine, but that death itself / was an inconsolable. / That no hideous key could be found / To unstitch its misery. / That any balm or philosophy was futile. / That its loop was infinite and precious / and impossible.' When we discover that 'precious and impossible' refers to death, another important theme is revealed in this volume. The deaths of both of his parents – Albert in 2017 and Janet in 1997 – are central threads. The looming specter of mortality and haunting memories inform a number of poems in an elegiac mode that commemorate the deaths of several friends and family members.

In addition to a superbly selected representation of poems from all five of Joseph's poetry volumes, *Precious and Impossible* closes with a rich and varied section of previously uncollected poems written in various periods and revised over time, and selected lyrics from Joseph's songs. The song lyrics, which share many of the same literary traits as the poetry, are nonetheless designed for performance and stress dynamic pauses, beats, and rhythmic and rhyming repetition. This final section adds a harmonising coda to the three decades of poetic craft represented in these pages. The inclusion of images throughout this book, such as the advertisements for each volume, intensifies the recognition of Joseph's prolonged career, dedication to poetry, and impact of the cultural context for each era.

Anthony Joseph has been writing with intensity and unique gifts for three decades. His blazing talent has always been evident along with an unwavering sense of his own journey through poetry and life. *Precious and Impossible* is a treasure that presents a major body of writing from a poet who has shown consistency in his influences, methods and goals from the start. The avant-garde has always been ahead of the game in revealing the hidden truths of its time and place, as we learned from innovators from William Blake to T. S. Eliot. As 'the leader of the black avant-garde in Britain', Joseph has been exploring and revealing a deeper reality for thirty years. If times and readers have caught up, it is all to the good. As *Precious and Impossible* shows, Anthony Joseph is one of the most important contemporary poets writing in English.

Lauri Scheyer earned a PhD from the University of Chicago in English and American Language and Literature. She is currently Xiaoxiang Scholars Distinguished Professor and founding director of the British and American Poetry Center at Hunan Normal University, China. She is also founding director of the Center for Contemporary Poetry and Poetics and Professor Emeritus of English, Creative Writing and Black Diaspora Literature at California State University, Los Angeles. Her edited and authored books include Theatres of War *(Bloomsbury),* A History of African American Poetry *(Cambridge University Press),* Slave Songs and the Birth of African American Poetry *(Palgrave Macmillan), and* The Heritage Series of Black Poetry *(Routledge). She also wrote the introduction to Anthony Joseph's novel* The African Origins of UFOs.

Endnotes

1. From 1990–1993, Joseph founded and performed in a rock group called Zedd. During that time, he composed a song using the phrase 'a ghost in the poison engine'. Though the song was never performed, Joseph thought that phrase would be a good name for a publisher by connecting poison with ink and engine with a printing press. With no financial backing and the added complication of featuring unconventional styles of literature, this collective enterprise was launched by Joseph with James Oscar, and later developed with Kemal Mulbocus and Keziah Jones. poisonenginepress also published Joseph's second book *Teragaton* (1997) and released his recording *Liquid Textology: Readings from* The African Origins of UFOs (2005).

2. Joseph was invited for return visits to Cal State LA which matched the resounding success of his 2004 residency. When I was appointed founding director of the British and American Poetry Center at Hunan Normal University in 2017, Joseph was invited to be the first British poet-in-residence to inaugurate the Center and had an equally dynamic impact on the Chinese audiences. His work is now part of the international curriculum in China, America and other world nations.

3. Although excerpts are not included in this book, the cover art for Joseph's first novel, *The African Origins of UFOs*, is a childhood drawing by his daughter Meena.

4. Correspondence to Lauri Scheyer, 2006.

5. This quotation appears on page 18 of Joseph's Introduction to the original publication of *Teragaton*.

Desafinado

1994

islands

scorched green
transparent air smell we breathe
waves
of stage script misery
weltering
of waves slapping waves

we islands
crossing rivers on stones

we islands
threw stones through
my paper marriage

but even in this eden
knives are drawn
speech rips
is transcribed
memorised

so memorise
the view
from the fort   the salt
in your eyes   the sea

the art of ageing

(for dennis)

my brother dennis
became a father first
last friday
he called collect
from five rivers
i wept
a cold sweat
wet
at the best news
i'd heard all year

dennis laughed
i laughed
we laughed
like children

on my bedroom wall hangs
a time stained monochrome
of finger sucking innocence
it even smells
of 1970
of toy trucks
of mud
of saliva
coconut oil
talcum powder and now

dennis says

write me
i say
send me

some photographs

clark boots

clark boots   rung
from beige Gabardine   bells

train set   coiled
in a cardboard   box
sittin' on topada   press

an' albert
tall to me
grins like flat cap

puts the train back

with a father's stretch

time
slipped
so to be sure
he filled
her pillow with
cherry blossom twigs
red shiny beads of
sweet orange pine
but
missed
'cause :
she could not
resist
the tongue that slid
sliding
a snake
he kissed
her lips
with aloe vera

the other frantically dialled
wrung her heart
to drip
honey
in the sun

he meanwhile lay confiscated
dyin' from the blues like robert johnson's shoes
bleedin' from a blues that
multiplies
like et ce   te   ra

constipated irises
dicks
of bread
french bread

crack pot
cum shot
blood clot

brass flavoured
irrelevants
rush
for the bus
to buy time
eating
a mars bar
rush
incognito
eating time
masquerading
as che
guevara

tea pot
screams babies
dribble
semen seeps
from rusty bibles
i
spin traffic
sixties marley
jorge ben's 'brother'

cafe regios
buddy miles an' lee michaels
band of gypsies and just like a baby

hallucegenic mouthpiece
metaphoric
inanimates
ammonia
in newsagent biscuits

play in the sunshine

hot sunday in may
peace park
hornsey rise

a blackbird swims
in figure eights
against a canvas
of cloud and sky

do clouds have names

a bold brass bee
stares me through my shades
zips
and flits
stares me again

maybe he writes poetry

west ken' winter

fast days for fast living days
the machinery of movement
wood green to west ken
via
mt. lambert
mind so fucked
i long for pleasure
like a fish
in a petrol tank

west ken' will break me
bleed me
my mansion
my house
my flat
is a room
18 x 12
my possesions
like cadavers
leave me a sometimes bed
never a desk
seldom a chair
always the carpet blackens my feet
cigarette soot like chalkdust
fills blackboard lungs
skin
as if nettle cursed
winter denuding
rags

stubble curls
are rehashed

as

christmas
carols down
fairholme road
i taste   i smell
i feel
without touch

my room
is 18 x 12
18 x 12 x 18 x 12

angels wearin' tens

in a room gaunt with
carnal overtime an' tone
temperature
of tepid celsius
love went
from 40 watts
to nakedness caressed
by rose petals drunk
with eucalyptus

velvet verbs
stutter
flutter
like crippled curtains
from rooms stained
with the skunk of sex

love leans
over
a hotel banister
pink nylon
satin
skin

trees

(for my mothers)

bare trees
tired with wintersleep

naked trees
like skeletons

bare bones of hands
reaching up like dead hands
tree bones

trees
with specks of buds
with march begins
to sprout

monsters
concrete ropes
that hang survival
from the bare navel
of existence

monsters
concrete ropes
that whip like flies
flies
that swarm
in stinging swarms
on flesh
that wears
like leather

monsters
graphite sling shots
that hit
like tyson

monsters
lucid germs
that swim
in the belly of
with crown of thorn haloes
that gash
in hard arpeggios

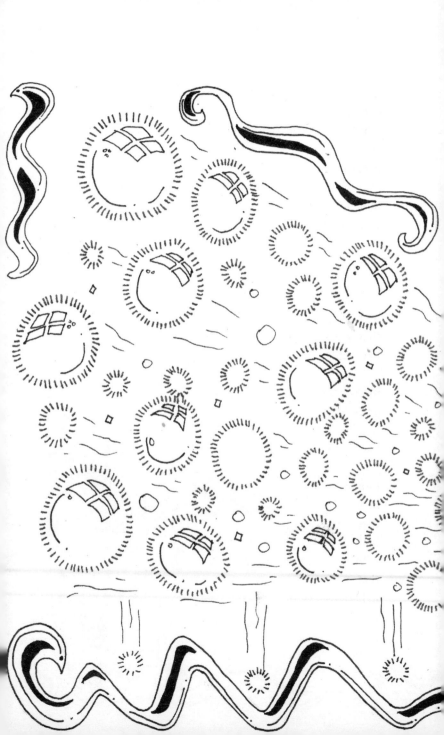

from a tie dyed vase
stained glass
rabid insipidity flings
spectacles of molten dust
clears 'is throat in mid throttle

BAWLS

like a tune up sax
wallet spills notes from prodigal moons
explodes in ecstatic nova of unmetred light
fluorescent d e t o n a t i o n of fluent hyperbole

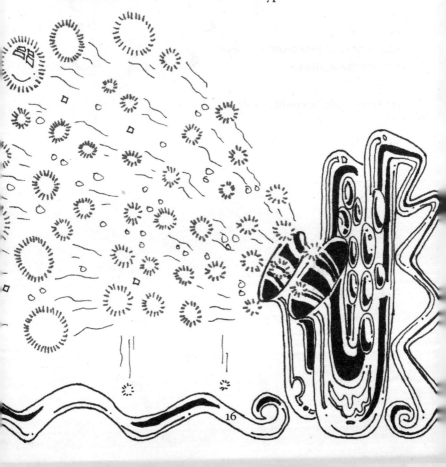

s a t u r d a y

(for zedd)

saturday

saturday

been dusted so long
it's not true

always
never compromise
and even trumpets blow
but not themselves

yes from critic to credit to east
to west end blues
we scanned
we surveyed
the usual streets
and tired bars

saturday became
saturday night

no brothers
on my sofa

naked in the mud
naked in the mud
father
i was a baby boy
were you

toy trucks
tractor wheels
and mother
swimming in the mud
swimming in the mud
of twilit
aranguez
savannah

tobago

on the panorama
through the gulf of paria
the caribbean sea
the salty white mist of ocean air
waves
as if razor whipped

tobago sun
tobago hot sand
pigeon point
white scorched and shimmering

i drive through terrain green with
hooded island rain forests
antique waterfalls
cocoa buttered banana fields

red heat
noon blaze
oiling my wave beaten bones
with coconut water and *vat 19*
as tobago mothers
rooted like earth
hawk from their stools
in head-ties and aprons

      tamarind balls
      an' sugar cakes
      twigs of spice

an' aniseed
leafs of *bambu* paper
loose cigarettes in jars

on a bleached veranda
of indian almond shade
a white beach
behind mt. irvine
i discuss island philosophy
with dreadlocked poets sprouting
black rock weed
night like the island's shadow

the light
tower cast
a lazy spotlight across a black harbour
as tobago
map of a hammock swung
between bent palms

e b b s
to sleep
watching the slow foam spray
of moonlit waves

poisonenginepress presents

TERAGATON
a book by Anthony Joseph

uncut phonetic funk,blacksurre st mbo
linguistic muscle,oblique word sculptures,a core-
text,abstract detonations of syntax,neolojismic
transliterations of intimate textology,an improvised
transcendental mantra,a script for grooving
tongues,freeform verse vernaculation, disembodied
poetic jazz, harmolodelic mouth-music for yourmind.

Spumatickumizajest!:*KeziahJones*

It is clear that Joseph has something
important to say, the task lies in
deciphering it :*Trace urbanmagazine*

Available at Dillons, Books Etc.,Tactical Cafe,Tower Records,
Blackwells,Compendium, Index Books etc. and by
Email:poisonenginepress@compuserve.com

design by granfads.backmouth

Teragaton

1997

b l a k d a d a m a s o n s o n g

for ted joans

mo`bone than gravediggerboots!
i eclipsed doped scopednscooped wt open palm
turnd to face the surf-
            surface of the moon

i came from blood wept rain an cum
swallowd entire oceans whole
carri/d m\muscle\n
russian armyhat warm
            wt blaksurrealistmanifesto btween elbows

            i sharpnd my toes
got deep suck sippin hot.orange juice in Gaza
red&wideeyed sniffin snaildung in Accra

my tongue super my tongue/bcome:
            spittin:
      OBEAH MANTRAS

i'll send a
lizard tippd spear tru
all cold froze rainbows you
    swallowd me whole you
        suckd me dry

europeisinmyass

dontsleeponyourbackyoullhavenightmareso
methingilearndformyselffictionispretensein
theroleoftheego4wordscallouscaseouscuntb
ushwasintranceshesveryeroticashesvery6r
ejectedwordsperfectriverpeacezincalloydisa
llowretrogradeifyoukeepwritingyoullbreaki
ntearsbroccolifishtearsassociativebehaviou
rcalmisuponmebtbigbooksLacanEcritswhat
willidothereisachapterontheletterintheunco
nsciousdescriptionsthesilverplatedscissoral
mosttouchestheteacupilostitifeltitgowasyes
terdayorganisetoothacheslowbuildinguntiln
extweekwhenitwasunbearablehadtogodenti
stwtaminerslampstapledtohisforeheadwrin
kledlipsfrmcrackedresonationsmesmerised
bysundaysoverheadmachineryundulatingbl
oodstreamburningbetweenthighsmypriceth
egestureremainsintactinsectveinspeechcon
formstoslenderlimbnumberssunsunsunmy
willisburnlittlefolkorbituaryfortheimagined
deadtaffiesweet+talked+goneheadbackande
yesstraightoutfrmnewspapereyeslookingov
ercheekbonebecausetheheadisheldbackbyth
edyingmoodalwaysasseveralsotightwalkrop
eingupacrossconcretevalleyholdingthembot
hfromfallintruwindowstheheadleansthefac
edripstheheadleansthefacedripsthefacedrip
smoltensolderdropsfallsl½ow¼lystretchingt
otheceilingofa4bedrmflatthesittingroomispav

edwtshingles&agueprofanity&colicstruggle
againstawindowwindowcrashestheyfallbaw
lasdownspinning4000feetaboveeyelevelmir
rorofinfinityfrmwheretheyfallevenskyscra
perslooklikemarginalsuicidesofbonsaimeat
windows2voiceerrorsalivatheslapwokemyw
akingswiftcutrushnoisejazzhissingfromstre
etbelowalgerianmarkettruecosmopoliticalsc
eneshearniggabawlintensifylooktruthewind
owsofthe13thfloorobservebriefcasegettingo
utoftaxitaxigettingoutofmanmangettingout
ofbriefcaseshelightsanotherthenwesiplemo
nionsyrupsameshitgavemearash2wksagon
owimsickagainriddimbusdestrategytraditio
ndictatesthatimustplaymydrumtalkingdru
mdancingwordssteppintosyllhypnotichipho
pmyriddimgobusdemstrategysureigotmyhe
adontighttootightsomoreblueswontpacifym
eriddimbusdestrategywelfarecustardinabo
wlonthekitchenfloorbulletrainastormoftear
sthemorewedisagreethemorewelovewelovec
isternbitchwhippulloutofcambodiacliponba
dgeofgeneralsamhocaughtbyredflashofrust
redwounddeepyellowhalothesuneruptsitisc
oldsocoldsointhispeculiarmotivemachinefig
htforpeacelipsofexcesscrypticpulsedripflux
recapitulativeconstantclingtofactorsofhone
stlybelievemeihavenotliedsimplydisturbed
myancestorsmasagenwalked80milesbutmy
eyesarefoldingawakeandtheswinginggatesd
raggrassscreamingbehindmethestenchthat
eruptsisofburntwatchbandsastrangerstong

uefingersmypalmiinspecttheticketwttheeye
stillwarmstillbreathingDJgunmanwassuspi
ciouswingsofnobodyahingeofbonebetweenfl
ammableflourescentorangemyskinflouresc
entgreenhescomingrosepetalsreleasetheirs
permcactusfrondsenclosestreetfunkhotred
burnbronzefromstonefromsteelremembert
he1sttimeyousawaghostsisawanapparition
ofobanhoytewalktrubothroomsinwhitewasc
aughtlaterthatnightwtmyfingersintocoinsfr
mdeoldmansshirtpocketbehindheglassescas
ebadbodybonebuckbreezebushbeardbruiseb
lessedbebergamotbackbonedropdeanchorw
alkupdatroadcarrycarrymyshieldofcrotons
pearsjunglebelowyellowjungleiwishyouwere
heretheredibisessitoutsidemywindowthewi
ndowsgoldenframeattractsevensnakesfrmt
hejunglebelowyellowjunglewhereeverythin
gsalwaysinseasondipmytonguedownmorni
ngsforpommecythere&mammyapplethemo
mentthatismissingistherevelationofthought
myhandsshookwhenistoodtheyaretheirown
theladywhochangesthesheetsisdressedlikea
nurseherpenisextendsunderherapronbuthe
rfacesoft&warmwhenitouchedherthenthec
urltriptiptopcrawlofaniguanacomingintomy
roomgettingintobedwtmeweeatboursinbeen
heresinceseptemberitseptemberagainconn
ectivedotsmyroomisapaintingofherebecould
youwishthoughtofrevelationisthemissingm
omentcrustaceanteaaffirmativepositionvie
wdownovercloudstrubarbwirewindowstosof

twhitecanvasahandrisesfrmtheblurcatches
thewingsinitsgripstirstheflyingmachinevo
mits29japanesetouristswttheirheadsinmac
ybagsmymentalselfmotiveisinmotionmotiv
atingchromesynchronicspuninswilltissuelu
ngfullofgrapesdestrictionstimespacetorotat
ecreateconvulsionsshifttherealoutoffocuscl
oudsonsanddisappearunderwherethesahi
ghwayfencedwt87moteldoorsambiguousbea
uty&eclecticmutationsplanetdreamstoostu
nkinblazetoforgettorememberwhowhatwhy
itwasgonebeforiarrivedonlyafragmentrema
insdattoodissolveslikesugarinsalivawhoisbi
llycampbellasnakeskindealerontheavenueo
ftearsaspit&shineshoehorninbriefcaseoftea
rsa2wonunchakukillerabscesspiercerjazzs
permcockburnshardfondledinmorningcolds
ocoldeventhumbtacksmoanmetabolicamp
hetamineuserwtthesunbrowntantheautoma
ticarmconcealedinherpurse1950s**austinca
mbridge**leatherstructureofboneinfingertip
protudingskintorninpulpofpusfiercemetalri
msofcentipedeinsectveinsheinsistsonlemon
greenicanntgivehermyloveisopentopersuas
ionirubthemagicpenejaculatesorangedyeshi
tshotacrossthehorizon2palmsteepleheldfir
mtoherbreastatmoaningplywoodjunctionha
llucinogenictonguetiptwistinginagonisingde
aththroesmyhandbrokeninvicegripunicornl
ipjazzsingerslipagainststereowindowdeathi
snotenoughthisshapeintowhichthedogsvoic
erepelsvisiontreewingtouchesoceanoceanw

29

erunindrowningunderseaarejewelsgoldbron
zebrassrimsofsilverchromeintensityahouse
crumblesinthedistanceimountmyhorsehors
esmadeofmetalsculpturefromscrapyardspo
kesformanesparkswegowetdustarmourweg
ohouseisburningburningtheyarecominghou
seisburningwegotruwindowsdonationscrapl
ightteleeyereflectingdonationhumangenom
eprojectcircular25bfingers10ankles2elbow
s2forgottenbody90%atanygiventimenose1b
ebopbrownstreet&crosswasthealleywher
edownwasdebebopwasdatsnatdatstraned
atsdizzdatsdextergordonsspeedona¼reedhe
uses2wontonguestoplay1inbody1ineheadblow
indeoriginalbawlthiscombustionproducesac
ryaJAZZwailalongkissonbrasslipstweeee
zealabamafirehumangenomeprojectcirc
ular25cbrain1mouth1tonguesmanyoneinm
outhmanyinheadblackintellectualsbuskinbr
ownsuitsguerrillawarfareisoutofprintsoimd
econstructingthesimulacramaticsituationso
fthisexistentialcollagewordbeatriddimiss
nakerubbertwistininabarrelwhowantstosw
apigotghostrider&doctorstrangefrom77luk
ecagewaspowermanin75blackpanhterfrm7
6bodykisscircumferencebodydiescomeagai
nviolentpampastrapmetalsoftnesschillieye
hairineyeoptrexeyewashsoftnessdeadbody
shiverjuptoSelDuncansmarinesqjazz1949u
mptoArtDeCoteauplayinmyfunnyvalentinei
nbossanova@seamen&waterfronthall1966j
eepfunkseranadesafricansfoxtrotinyorube

ahnightdruminhillsaboveportofspainbuckn
eckcannibalismindisroomwereonthetvni
ggaschewindeyfingerboneseatingourselves
thisbloatedcorpselikesewerlakepuffdeat
hcraterfleshgrainyporouslumpskinshealso
ateherselfshowingusboldlyhervisciousssig
httrulynudecomebackcomebackcomba
ckifadeinkfingerswetpaintedirisoftruepigm
entofblackhoneyrapidlipsofmiricles&dustb
readthecityappearstobebuiltonplateauxit
isoratleasthighuphillslookout&seasee

itsover

camel, a small painting

camel a small painting,the so called 'white lady'
(opposite) the tiv are renowned as thatchers, blier
1987- a veritable hypocaust. akua ba.it has been-
fanti doll clearly suspended frm his neck, or
libel.140.141 wooden-terracotta, nok culture–
bronze-clearly defined. infantile although–
the face is bearded. fetish lids, an imported mirror-
the fewer-the lid,himself-the lids vary in
complexity. some sculptures are kept wrapped–
the fierce body.we removed its garments-fetish
figure, nine days later to be burned-small pox-
african mask-monoxylous, ie. to represent water-
out of a single block of wood-mask of identical
appearance. bayaka eyes and the elbows on knees-
mythical creates-obo ekiti,
cassava, lobi-modern place names-woman
holding a fan (now bent) rubin-ht.45½ in.oron.l.
8½ in.camel,a small painting

t i n c t u r e

a red sun the size of belmont rises over jerningham avenue
its rays are webs are ladders to every street here
                        the red
                      bronze/
              steelpansticksonfire-gold
              smell of fresh paint
          on the midnight robbers collection box

                              khakibootsblew frm 2nd avenue

                    tincture

                  bright orangegreen
                with the red of hibiscus scent
              over the blacktonguewoman fence
          & her beardeddaughter their
                  windows tied wit steel

the sun risen also rises here frm it down one of its
ladders

                                    a figure appears

the buff

for my father

they believe in electricworkmen here they give them
wine the compressed fear of the
stairway that leads down krik
                            krak
it was about
                    computing

5Dimensional objects appear to bulge from the hand
held screen

rain drowns the traffic

umbrellas aswideas latrine roofs lashing raincuffs the
knees of me

bt albert what did i do you told me the next time i you
how *i* felt
an there was tenderness there
on that watery mountain

a guava tree

for my mother

her breasts were sore i'd seen her years before
as shouting woman behind the fence and the orange
tree across the green frm walking 2nd avenue.she was
such a modern poet then bt now she appeared to see
the doctor.

i listened to dem bitch it got dark out in de shed.still
wt her & she teacupbreasts which pained her waiting.i
knew then how it would end.

the guava tree is fruitless this year i'm here.is:cut
out/down/rootburnt was my best friend in the
yard.ok.the orange tree reached the roof and the
savannah view frm hot galvanise and the avocado trees
bt you were different.

so seeing.the guava tree burndead last july and the
doctor she also dead then the screams which came
from inside the house made me realise that dat that dat
whole chapter of my life was
deadburn/burndead&ended(off.like
psychictravel silverspine gut cut
then neverness

genealogy.became ash with the burning brain
of 74yrs history ws bury/d and then 48 i cant explain
but the sadness it came.without stopping to see where
my friend had been cut&burning murder.

The bedroom doors are lockd shes waiting.with her
lump in teacup waiting to see the doctor bt.i
already know how this will end.

from the bedroom come tears & please-he wants to go
she begs him no-grinds more tears frm her eyeballs

he stands the bed creaks he stands he wears
brown.shortsleeved indiansilk sits in the cornr fixes hs
boot.there is no music here/an abcess of colour.

drab curtains/pumkin orange walls bt the old woman's.
ornaments in place.the laminated chest of drawers.the
dining table.the dove-brown 3piece suite- the
photographs on the wall will be turnd around. even
Ursula at 25.beautyfull bust of the princess.her
dress.appears to be sequined.it is.&pink.her eyes
permanently southwest profiled has been there since
1970

surrender
he's leaving
he is
he's leaving
he
he's leaving
he is
he's gone)

the roof heaves wt   oldwoman heaving.bleeding tears
into her anturium dress.
crying so that my heart twists   helpless.the shouting

stops suddenly silent.

then she leaves
and i'm not sure
how it'll end anymore.

indian red

i get lost in strange city.this actors swimming pool is his bathtub in the yard.in this episode he is interviewing a blackwoman.spins on his swivell hires her.nxt scene they are in bed.all this time with a wooden map of the caribbean nailed to his back. teragaton.

a special dog and these english rites.he's never been in this special building.special building has red carpets which are exclusive to all bt beefeating upperneckers. however-they allow the dog.today.

i arrive at work and everyone wants to buy me drinks but then I go cruising and the dog interlude.the actor's my father unmasked as myself at his age.we waltz down the bellbottom streets and through hills of musk in a dim-moon valley.

i arrive at work and everyone-my boss.she's standing in the doorway.i'm ½ a day late.adrian brings me a bottle of babashbushrum-tells me where everyone is.2 round back fixin instruments

tell her i'm vrrysrry.she's very femme fatale standing in the doorway smoking a cigar and doesn't fire me.tell her this shirt in my bag is the
only shirt i have with me.today.

shirt of my favorite funk.indian red

.teragaton

garden

listening to portable jungle in a wet garden beside a
flooded river.earlier the river claimed lives-we saw it
live-there were children-crushed against a boatside
while news of the carnival spread by radio

rusty blues man McKlutchie was a tailor by day-this
evening saw him sharpening his guitar strings-he came
down to the harbour

they died screaming-until their screams died too

we thought-it mustve been McKlutchie-twisted muscle
of night-making plans to meet trinidadians in plywood
fete that night-but out all day and then she wanted
to go home - change

B   i   g   7   0   s   h   i   g   h

tigerbalm

sketching dust slowmotion step across bone desert
into shapes - one which
lights the wheel
the spasm exposes the truculence of memory
pushes the cart of noises beyond
the 15eenth of everything
a cutlass falls spinningspinning falls spinning
tru the tents striped apex it
divides the now silent conversation

bu(t
win)d
moan(ing
wt)
hunger
(blows
our
eyes
o(ff

she brings us tea we exchange alibis
confuse the jury refute all sensibility
exteradicate all evidence bt our armpits
have swallowd

BENGUE'S BALSAMIC OINTMENT

ignites tarpaulin

fire runs burning down
running hill down burning

the river starts here

ripples cold
caress the water

rivers hair
longer than

bird wing startles morning

black&white dark shadows

used to stay up to watch
𝕯𝖆𝖗𝖐 𝕾𝖍𝖆𝖉𝖔𝖜𝖘
wt m'grandmother.1975
after 11-de ol`man snorin-
me an she on de couch me
btween she toes watchin
𝕭𝖆𝖗𝖓𝖆𝖇𝖆𝖘 𝕮𝖔𝖑𝖑𝖎𝖓𝖘

white face sharp bone pointy collar
    black coat&cape stiff devil teeth-dem fangs
-double incisors that sunk
      into the flesh of de swooning neck
                  behind de straight black

bt de dagger had de villain f'Barnabas
        lyin in a coffin

all   light off in de house

dogbark&fridgehum she dead&gone
                  me
                     in dark shadows

wildlife

for james oscar

1
cafe.the living room.soho 9.30.
we are words writing themselves
our lips move like pens extend as fingers
(text&con.text.)
`*form is what happens*`

Bateman st.Rasa Sayang.loreli.
breath-fire-air
most abundant always more
(affect & effect.)
pause.another cigarette.

2
a piano seduces a memory
waves&sand crash   against stone
(ero or corosion)

The Thunderstone: *my grandmother believed*
these fell from the sky.they did.
                    i realised years later   they were
                            meteorite particles.

Testing the Thunderstone:
tie wt thread the smooth black stone found in the

sungreen savannah.
allow to hang-a pendulum
stab wt fire-
the stone should not fall

a scorpion in a crease of brown pine.
burn between scissors then eat limbxlimb
(antidote against its sting)

an iguana in our backyard.
when we killd it we found
eggs in her stomach

ting

soundtrack: betty davis/70sblues

in a hot brown field in a shack with abeautyfull woman
in the field a house of drawers behind us a stadium
where from our frontdoor sunshade reflects sprinters in
grainy close up of blue thighs flashing

our ct/au/dg is long legs wear stockings

bukka white/aberdeen mississippi blues

we run frm the horned wild boar wt the shaggy fur over
the chicken wire her white dress exploding

new location: Mitagua Junction.3am

a woman acrss the sidewalk her head against the wall
she has a jericurlafro which bleeds a bloodstream into
the street she tells me why when I walk past the 2nd
time

behind the wall is a hospital emergency unit where the
pharmacy used to be biglights a volkswagen ambulance
the receptionist shows me

brownchildrenonotherchildrensbicycles

tells me to walk the bleeding home to Mitagua which
is a village up the hill to our left the bleeding agrees
already up and walking/holding
her head

45

i tell the receptionist

bukka white/pinebluff arkansas

*i'd take a cab bt i'm broke till i get paid
tomorrow*

we laugh she gives me 3£s

where was i coming frm the stadium an
australian desert running from beasts
the university

are you.a communist

bukka white/the panama limited

teragatonic sampling

asafoetida

surround your awareness
wt awareness for your surroundings

exhaling   trees bent with my
blink.clouds went

                                            down

        in new hat bt nobody notices

    bandagedglasseslady bought 1 small Baileys & 1 rum

2hrs sleep cant keep my eyes open all i need is my nose
open
everything else is a luxury

there were dramastic changes-woman on ch4 pot
debate

                        well i been smoking cannabis for 40yrs-
                        Kris Krishna in the audience

missing part of New York Storys

we took the F train to
LAFAYETTE&BROADWAY
brownsteelstairways

```
DO SPORT
NOT DRUGS
PAY TOLL
```

deepfriedduckling&tofu*NewHungWongHouse@*
212 grand
roi jones collected prose&plays
dexter gordon&memphis Queen

sittin in Times

```
bitin the bride

a dog walks past

in tshirt&scarf
```

THE MUSEUM OF MODERN ART

jacob lawrence:the exodus
boccioni:unique forms of continuity in space
marcel jean:spectre of the gardenia
barnett newman:RED
andre breton:poem object
alberto giacometti:woman with her throat cut

jazz crusaders:new time shuffle

SUSPEND REASON
i walked across the room
SUBSTITUTE TIME
i'm not sure now
if i'm insane or near to
destruction.i must be.
will my nose bleed. i'm dancing. wt fire
when vice grips my skull
between cartilage&cranium
eyes waiting to burst at any moment
at any & every at once
(forgetin wot i supermarket needs frm)
(slam glassing)
(broomstick metal smashing)
(idiolectophobia)
(cyclothymia)

id.'id,(psych.)n.the sum total
of the primitive instinctive forces
in an individual subserving
the pleasure/pain principle.

BASIC REQUIREMENTS
medicine
warmth
mediation
buddha
jesus
allah
jah
bodhidharma
jazz
sex
subversive poetics
intimate meditation in a hotel room
Écrits

J.O.
the writer has been living here since march.he has 8
luggage & assorted bags back to montreal
earlier i saw him frm the minicab we ran 8 flights
up.turning the key the whole lock fell out.the writer
had to prise a lever wt a screwdriver while i held
matches

the plants on the window ledge have not been
watered since may no sense of human presence besides
the writers musk.tonight after the hottest day so far
this summer.

how i could stop smoking:
if i read that smoking affects yr writing

at such moments the conscious and unconscious
conspire to provide the maximum effect

UNDIVIDED MIND

how to write

core/teragatonic substance
⇩
unconscious
⇩
conscious-for scrutiny
⇩
unconscious -for final synthesis
⇩
signal to conscious that synthesis is done
⇩
writing begins

however
it is possible
to write directly frm center

pure thought as oppossed to first thought

coffee

after just 2 wks of writing into morning
i am already filled with such pain
ready to exhale tears

the problem of being must take precedence over that of knowledge

haiku 1

all afternoon putting out stock
wondering if i bought the right colour shoe

How to write

set clock for 6.15 write 3 pages
make cartoon demon put an X tru it.

art may seem to spring frm pain
bt perhaps this is because pain
focuses our attention on detail

images

sketch as opposed to picture

a pair stroll pass in full 40s american gothic
hs smooth
beige
sharp zoot suit straw
fedora
cigar
creased ol'plastic gangster face
bt hs eyes were f$@%@*WILD

her thin
grip
waist rollin jellyroll
arse deep
stilettos
dark sunglasses bouffantblonde
wt her metal purse

'i bought them by weight
800 lbs of books'

haiku 2

jasmine scent from chinatown teapot
mingles wt midday heat

keep your mind in hell,
and despair not-_{Staretz Silouan}

iamblacksurrealist

Ted Joans

thought defined in the absence of all control exerted by
reason…outside all aesthetic or moral preoccupations

yoz & the clapham pizza incident

every friday rudy & mohammed would argue about
money tonight they started in the kitchen behind
the oven badpay every friday they would argue
tonight rudy coulda bust the glass he holding in
m'mmed face but Yoz is de badpay & bossman to
kill for shortmoney friday Rudy & Mohammed would
argue but tonight …

How - not - to write

3 crossrhymed iambic pentameter quartrains
followed by an iambic pentameter couplet
as opposed to
an octave consisting of 2 quartrains with the same rhymes in envelope
fashion then a sestet employing 2 or 3 more rhymes

NOT LIKE BUT IS

morning.redsmeared filter of a woman's cigarette
porcelain cowhead between lettuce green peppers
& carrots
limbless blonde mannequin torso hung frm shop
window ceiling

the evolution of pure mental representation in the
plastic arts is due to the invention of
photography.
Photographic eyeballs
graphic arsehole revealers

the reptiles skin is chrome its mouth a cool wound

ParanoiacCriticalActivity:
spontenousmethodofirration
alknowledgebaseduponthein
terpretativecriticalassociati
onofdeliriousphenomena

haiku 3
sunday morning
butcher's apron on a wall

60

vervain with kimono

the succulent womb broken glass cas)

cading

tru waterfall of violet hair-was(

p

meat decoding telegraphic cunt

sulphuric yellow
brass jukebox jazz

iamtheinterplanetarypostman

madness

mouthfulla splinters

lungfulla grapes

better be mad than sorry

is the word long,will intended readers understand
the word is the word
necessary

meanwhile back at the bookshop

ol'sicilian spy he ask:
'where for concealed book book look like book
bt wt hole-conceal document put in library'

2 bearded bros. ask me
for books by Hitler

yellowface

awareness of the I
reflected in the mirror confused
your image wt mine

carbide

Distance & Disengagement

paranoia of being is you are in this bodything
which represents you
-who is this bodything-
we cant see how we're seen is paranoia of being
the ego revealer
bt in the absence of a face or if i wore a mask
i could walk through the city naked

they race faster than caustic bush

bt they embrace rather than crush

we no longer communicate

even the hidden skin when in-the deep

sleeps in a sea of mirrors

2. vertical essays on surfaces using photos of walls & streetwise iguanas

3.jury sees photo of victim's skull

4.'freedom is freedom from the need to be free'

5.'you are who you pretend to be'

6.perilous envy of impossible shoes & amphibious bracelets

7.ma's new girl beats wang wins nealus milikings

8.HIDs/metal halides 400(Mhz) sodium vapour

9.new gizmo traps thieves inside your car
and kills them

10.spirit lash finds tattooed armchair wt bobtail
deception

11.zoot allures shows Zappas'gunsack

12.dry bone lucidity expressed in the caseous underlung
of bionic poets

13.hardcore nigga in erection boots swallows
burning bus f' flesh

14. SUBAQUATIC EQUILIBRIUM

Such.what ride?this interface/the first pillar of
decisive temporality-beyond the serpentine
aroma which carves a halo of smoke chambers
for dwelling-so unkind to   black folk

the imagined eye sees the country's rush
reflected in the speeding windows-we go deeper
into a sea of grass in a pumpengine jitney

/extending out to brightness

in kandahar village tru the bushy hills-no one
told me there were grecian ruins here-a
sprawling metropolis of rotting stone-a
pantheon,a statue of hercules in a pool of green
water surrounded by corinthian pillars

falling tru water into darkness with africa's ease

standing on a hill overlooking the stone

17. HOW TO BUILD A TIME MACHINE

timeflight by spacelabour/alternatives to fuelrockets/explosion/propulsion» 25th century/ portable anti-proton tractor/accelerator/speed of light=built in speed of universal limits-beam laser reflection/matter/anti-matter detonation system-collision of anti-matter/anti-matter/time slows down the faster you move-1 millionth of a gram of anti-matter to mars and future/separate magnetic metal twins wt the power of an exploding star /force of virtual con+dis connection creates wormhole/jump into worm hole wearing african spaceboots.

9

we were about to have sex she had a face that had been
crying
she said she
would not be able to come
that she'd used all her water for tears

The Jazz Crusaders Live
in *New York*

i looked tru my 509 albums fo`Jazz
skimmin brimmin
sweet Jazz
street Jazz
sparklin Jazz
ripplin Jazz
bt i was low
        on jazz an`
Ramsey Lewis wont do
create that late
friday night
alone bt for
Jazz Coltrane dear old
Stockholm
one down one up

blow!

even Oscar Peterson wont blend wt these orange walls

i wanted to
get in touch
with strong prose i chose
`roi jones:**blackmagicpoems**
`cause tonite.tonite is no
Capt.Beefheart.not tonite is no
Chick Corea.not tonite is no

Canned Heat.no.tonite is no
tonight is
sardine a la carte`n
ornettedextergordonduke
Ellington
no blues jus`Jazz
skimmin brimmin 52nd
streetJazz sweetJazz
sparklin niggaskin ripplin Jazz

no blues
no blues
no more blues

THE PRAGUE POST

N&D
NIGHT AND DAY
June 16 – 22, 2010

ANTHONY JOSEPH & THE SPASM BAND

Hot sounds at the Respect Festival **B3**

MUSIC John Mayall talks about the blues **B5** **STAGE** Massive Attack, back on track **B7**
RESTAURANTS American kitsch gone bad **B10** **FILM** A passable *Prince of Persia* **B14**

Bird Head Son

2009

Conductors of his Mystery

for Albert Joseph

The day my father came back from the sea
    he was broke and handsome.
I saw him walking across the savannah
    and knew at once   it was him.
His soulful stride, the grace of his hat,
    the serifs of his name
      ~ fluttering ~
        in my mouth.

In his bachelor's room in El Socorro that year
he played his 8-tracks through a sawed-off speaker box.
    The coil would rattle an the cone would hop
but women from the coconut groves
    still came to hear
    his traveller's tales.

Shop he say he build by Goose Lane junction.
    But it rough from fabricated timber string.
      Picka foot jook wood
    like what Datsun ship in.

And in this snackette he sold   red mango,
    mints and tamarind.
Its wire mesh grill hid his suffer well tough.
    Till the shop bust,
      and he knock out the boards
      and roam east
      to Enterprise village.

Shack he say he build same cross-cut lumber.
    Wood he say he stitch same carap bush.
Roof he say he throw same galvanise. He got
    ambitious with wood
        in his middle ages.

That night I spent there,
        with the cicadas in that clear village sky,
even though each room was still unfinished
    and each sadness hid. I was with
    my father
    and I would've stayed
    if he had asked.

Brown suede,
    8 eye high
    desert boots.   Beige
gabardine bells with the 2 inch folds.
He was myth.   The legend of him.
Once I touched the nape of his boot
    to see if my father was real.
Beyond the brown edges of photographs
    and the songs we sang
        to sing him back
            from the sweep and sea agonies
                of his distance.

Landslide scars. He sent no letters.

His small hands were for the fine work of his carpentry.
        His fingers to trace the pitch pine's grain.
            And the raised rivers of his veins,

      the thick rings of his charisma,
            the scars — the maps of his palms —
   were the sweet conductors
               of his mystery.

Aiyé Olokun.

He came back smelling of the sea.

Bosch's Vision

It started as I was leaving
   with a dim groan in the afternoon.
I saw my grandmother
   embrace me
      in her hand stitched dress
   and wrench my soulcage open.

I saw vistas of apocalyptic Europe,
     heard obscure tongues.
       Till sudden now the sky become
      peppered with woe.
Slack eyed soldiers were howling
      in the wind.
Botched leper experiments
     and gene mutations
     with veins hung
     like vervain from the neck.

The sun long gone and weeping.

    The oil.

    The Devil.

    No doubt it was.
    The Devil.
    Who chased colour from the earth.
       Who left sulphur where he spoke
        like a jitney carburettor.

No doubt it was.
    The devil.
    Twisted muscle of night.
    Who crackt
    the sky glass lid.

    Maman.
Tell me again why I should leave this island.
Tell me again that those cities exist.
        All I know of the ocean
           is that a river
             starts here.

The day I left Mt Lambert
    the wardrobe doors would gleam.
It was a day like any other.
      Woodslaves ran and woodslaves waited.
      Lovers lay against the Samaan trees.
      Cattle grazed and bachacs burned
        in matchbox discotheques.

    But we were going to the airport
and my brother in the backseat
        is him I ask : *is me*
        this happening to?

Punk

I used to have a ponytail
twisted with beeswax to bud until
it curled like a scorpion's tail.
I uses to twist it and tug it to grow it,
but it grew so slow it got shaved.

I used to have a punk
short front and sides,
the back fat — I used to grease it —
with curl activator — to wave it
but it still sprung tough like spring.

One Saturday (cause Saturday was always
the day for cutting hair)
the barber asked me 'How yuh want it?'
and I said 'High top fade'
cause I was almost grown.

But when I got home the old bull flashed
some serious leather in my waist. He said
'What kinda kiss-me-arse cut is this?'
an took me back same time to the barber
to get my head shaved.

Sylvia

Birds and their talons
have sea in their sadness
and sky in the roof of their mouths.

And in old Mt Lambert
the rooms are dishevelled
      and silent

      she left

with her hair tied
wearing a dress of orchids,
looking back
from a photograph I took
      on a sepia avenue.

Sophocles

The pietà I saw
was where the rain
burst through
a hole in the wall
and my grandfather and four strong men
their black skin splashed
by the water rushing
pressed hard against
the hinge of its gush
and tried to stress it shut
But the water rushed
too strong and they cried
louder
than the storm itself
with the ruthless rain against them
and the glimpse I stole
stayed permanent
like a painting

Bermudez

for Noel Ramirez

The gold ring blinks on the barber's crooked thumb
as he sharpens his razor, with slapping strokes on leather,
strapt from the drawer in which he keeps his fee
and his brushes in his hairy aviary
behind the tyre shop, near Bermudez biscuit factory
with its cinnamon air, where we pull kites across
the old train tracks, and you
singing high in your heaven with each whip of the tail.
It is here, between the river and the sandbox tree
that I see you most, walking
past the black tongued witches' house,
past the stables through the brittle heat of the savannah,
steep from running sideways fastest,
hunting snakes and strange fruit.

The Carnival Suite

1
Snow drives down from the north.
The raindrops before the snow fell
seemed to fall slower
to the ground.
Then a woman in the bakery said
                              'Is that snowing?'
But not yet.
It is Ash Wednesday so I know
                    the carnival is over.

2
round de savannah on carnival tuesday
      first go by Garib mas camp
            where dem rich gyal does stay
an bass does rattle all yuh rib an teeth
                        an we sippin
            somethin cold
watchin the DJ slap slide down
      he up in the veranda grinnin
      crab ways sideways when jus so he drop some vincy
            riddum
an people start bawl an dey waist rip roll
      but dat young gyal in she tight-tight jeans
            the one who feel she hoity-toity
      with she barbecue wings and she Carib shandy
      who does dance like she wearing high heel
            we does see she an she sister all bout town
                  like freshwater yankee

```
                    leave she dey man
            doh even try — unless you name is Jamada
                            you
                            cyar
                            jam
                            dat!
        dem so does only want man with motorcar
                to wine on dey bumsee


                    lord a wonder where las-lap go ketch we tonight
        If las lap ketch we here by Cipriani Boulevard
                with all dem ma commère man
                we eh go feel free
                is real jam we need
                leh we go by green corner
                        where dem real yard fowl does be
                leh we go
                    up in de harp a de congo
                    where Scipio an Gunta does be
                leh we go round by south quay
                        down Mucurapo Road
                        round Roxy roundabout
                        where dem long time jammete does be.
```

3
Beat my brother with a guava wood cane.
Beat him but he will not speak.
Is like
he not
glad to
see me
till I catch rage

and cuss from both sides of my mouth
and hurl tight fists an fingernail his face.
Beat my brother with a guava wood cane.
Cause all he brings are dry words
that quiver to dust
in the chaos parade
of masqueraders
passing us by.

Salt in my eyes.

He does not soothe my love.
His will not meet my gaze.
Beat my brother with a cocoa tree branch.
But when we embrace
> *O Den-Den, my nigger*
> *my brother,*
> *my blood*

:: Night is shaking
feathers shut
behind us ::

4
Jourvert mornin mud mas
in the jungles of Port of Spain
and my brother sips sugarcane brandy
on the East Dry River bridge.
Then we roam a thicket of brimful streets
    through town
in search of
    Saturnalian ointment.

Let us travel dangerous routes
where cut-eyed boys are waiting
to feed us puncheon rum
an learn us how to spit between thick thighs.
Let us follow this spirit procession
past the jetty where fish gut and shrimp stalk
wash up and stinking
in a stagnant black moss
where sequined spears are floating.

Blockorama

for Ronnie McGrath

stand leaning dusk
     in bland synthetic night
          pot hounds
          chicken hawks
          red dirt dregs and drains
          with my head hung
          in paraffin yards   tack mud
          gravel pits and dog shit alleys
          between wood shacks for road

I saw her from across the street I saw her in cadmium red
I followed her to the junction
with my hard jazz finger

She stepped out
     — 2 seater sports
          her afro took the whole top curve
          to stride — flail of colours —
          to a man stood in a doorway
          stroking his hick an oily beard/red
          green gold dashiki
          pitch oil light
          lamp the hill tracks coming down
          and a crowd start to build and guggle
          in the basketball fields down Goose Lane
          El Socorro
          to rock to real dubroot rockers like

Louie Lepki and BB Seaton

Roam strolling slick
>   in foreign suede
>>   through rhyming island country
>>   Through vines of poor folk roads
>>   rustic in the marigold
>>   My boots are hollow
>>   Her shoes are tallow soled

Seahound of an orchid
>   a trumpet
>>   a mouth like the blues
>>   and mellow greens of Sunday morning
>   evangelical
>>   soft leatherette
>>   brass goblets of salvation   Water
>>   where gusts overtook these humble
>   chambers
>>   and how a simple glance of light
>>   could bruise the island's southern road
>>   She did always sing
>>   seen her before
>>>   sing across the black ravine

Bird Head Son

for Kamau Brathwaite

1

At some dusk burning bush
in the back
yard fowl raking in
the dust dirt an soot
Gripe-green guavas and iguanas
lime tree root
bare naked fruit
of Pomme-cythere an Zaboca

The Sikyé fig and the green plantain
The old man in his Wellingtons
with his cutlass stabbin in
the soft dirt beside the dasheen stream
Its blade glint ** sparks **
colonial iron
colonial black
rubber heel

The leaping tongues of flame
that plead with the darkness to wait
Night is a secret a promise to keep
What burns
in the black pepper soot
of leaf and feather
when he fans the flame?

2

An dat guava tree root dat burn too
De same guava tree dat used to bring out she young — hard an
    green.
Then when de rain come it pulp would glow — it sweet get soft
an it stem get slippery to release the yellow beads of its honey

Well all I could do when I see it that year
was to seek it beating heart
where the fire never reach
A never ask why
When you shivering with sickness in your wicked room
an you motorcar park up an you false teeth rot
an dat same jumbie vine dat you tired kill
still reach in
creep in

Even these trees will die
Even the weaves of beetles and red ant gullies
and the underground streams that trickle will not
Even the sweet Julie mango tree is weeping white lice

Between this spirit bush — a see a Iguana —
sat still in the midday sun with it eye up
an it belly puffin tender

As quick as it is not enough to escape
the stick that breaks its back
Till its spasm is dire
And its mouth becomes a poem   with no words

3

Yuh ever wake up one Sunday mornin
an walk round yuh cassava?
Inspect yuh lime tree
for aphid
yuh dasheen
see how dey growin
An you frizzle neck cock
jus kickin dust back an crowin

You ever ask yuhself
what snake is this lord
dat leave this skin?

You ever walk out in dem Indian garden
an see a aeroplane passin
an imagine
is you in it
dat leavin?

When you never even row boat
an you navel string tie-up tie up in dis aloes bush
An all dem crapaud an lizard that making mischief
know your name

And all dem saga boy still grinning coins on Mt Lambert
        corner
see you when you pass an asking
        'Ai, you is bird head son?
You mus be bird head son f'true
        cause your father head
                did small too.'

The Tropic of Cancer

Glimpses of her
in insufferable light
        from the pitch pine root
            of a wooden room
                beneath
                    the tropic of cancer

Up past the bedsprings and coconut coir
and see her walking
        past a window
where curtains bloom
        in the paraffin night

    Glimpses of her
        tearing polyps from her heart
        by the burnt cedar saw mill on Jogie Road
            with the red dust grain
                    at dusk — her face
            pressed against a gate
                that would not swing

In Ramkisson Trace with the muddy drains
            I saw her once
burn a thorn from her heel
        with a candle's blade. In those days.
In those days my mother lived
in a two room apartment beside a mountain
        with water-soaked wood stuck in the mountainside.
Where she washed her pans and feet

                  was ochre brown
                        where the ground
                                  was slippery

         At Caura River I see her burn
                  sugar in a black iron pot
         bamboo jungle an creek
                  where the river was dark
                              beneath
                  the tropic of cancer

Yet later I remember her more clearly
detained in airport mystery rooms
         with her bag and soft possessions
                  Or among the yellow narcissi
                        in Hornsey Rise that winter
                  with her lump in tea-cup waiting
                  and her wig and beads
         in a hell of hot tears

Mr Buller

Mr Buller seep out sudden
    from deep Cantaro bush
        and it was the talk!
      But how Ma Daisa
        in she seventies
  could come jus so
        an marry a man like he
    in these late seventies?
An dance castilian
    in Hilton ballroom
      with this frog face man
who smell like black an white lizard shit
    and spootin spit
an come from cocoa country
      in that baggy brown suit
    an he garrulous mousche
an he bandy two knee
    with he hernia heng low
        Who spoke drunkwise,
          who could transcribe?
No, his whole head shook when he spoke
and words would roll round his jaw and stay loose
    as if booze
      had them bazodee.

But Buller had a stash of Atlantic 45s
in a broko down cabinet bottom
    — was the pure jump
      rhythm an blues!

But he'd cuss if anyone ever touched his Joe Turner
      an he'd lick down for Ruth Brown.
          He'd bark for Fats Domino —
                              no no no!

   And if you just as touch he Ray Charles
                      or he Earl Bostic slides;
      he lock off the draw
      one time.

Bougainvillea: Super 8 Red

KING CARNIVAL
    YUH HEADPIECE SO HEAVY
    SO SLOW TO WALK
      WITH THIS
        COSTUME BEHIND
     AS IF IT BUILT WITH
       YOU IN IT

    MIDDAY NEAR MEMORIAL PARK
     IN SUCH MERCYLESS HEAT
AND THESE BLUE HILLS
    THAT RIM THE CITY
 TRUCK BORNE
      SOUND
    OF ICARIAN TRUMPETS
A REAM OF HORNS
   A RHYTHM SECTION
    BEATS IRON INTO
      SOUND

   OX BLOOD AND FIREBRICK

   RED

SUCH BLOOD   BEADS OF SERPENT
   PURPLE
  BEADS AND BELLS AND TEETH
    THAT SHIMMER BLAZE
  DOWN

                    FREDERICK
                              STREET
THRONGS AS THICK AS
      WET GRAVEL

  SUPER 8 RED
    AND BURNT CLAY
BEARDS
    DIFFUSED AND REFRACTED
            INTO LIME GREEN
                              LAMÈ   LUMINOUS
                EYELETS IN
                    MAD BULL
      MASKS
                    CADMIUM RED OR
            LILAC PALMS
      A SCEPTRE HE HOLDS
            NEMO
        SHONE BLACK AGAINST THIS
            GLITTER
    DIAMANTE AND FRIVILOUS
      FEATHERS
            GLIMMER
ON HIS FACE
                    WET AND
SUPPLE IS HIS IDIOM
                    SWEAT
AND ENDLESS TECHNICOLOUR PRAYERS
      O MOTHER OF PEARL WITH
      SCENT OF FRESH PAINT WIRE BENT

WHICH EMBLEMS ARE THESE
                    RIVER GODS WITH
SUCH RAMPANT PLUMAGES
        STARTLING IN
THE FIRESKY

THE MOKO JUMBIE
        12 FOOT UP
                STILTS OF WOOD
        PAINTED WHITE/WHITE
        PAINTED WOOD
                    SLACK
            BRUISED WHIP OF HIPS THAT
            KEEP TIME
ALL THESE
                    COLOURS
                THAT DRIP FROM HIS FACE
                HIS APPOLLIC BUST
                        MONOXYLOUS
            TO REPRESENT WATER
                    OBATALA OR SPIRITUAL
                    BAPTIST

                THE MUD BAND STRETCHED THERE
            FROM G TO B FLAT
            ON KEATE STREET
OUTSIDE DELUXE CINEMA
            WAITING
FOR CHARLIE'S ROOTS
                TO PASS
                SO MUCH TAR GET JAM
            ON THAT BARBERGREEN

SO MUCH BLOOD SPUME
FROM THEM STEEL WHEEL
OF STEEL   BAND   PUSHING
DOWN FROM HILLTOP
ROLLING BASS DRUM
ACROSS THE DUST AND BIG YARD
STAGE

WE USES TO RUN
FROM OIL AND TAR BAND
LONG TIME
BURROKEETS
AN DEM JAB MOLLASIE
DEVIL MAS
FROM CASABLANCA BADJOHN
AND HELL'S YARD CATELLI ALL-STARS PAN MAN
FROM DR RAT AND RENEGADES
AND ALL THESE WARS
THAT MUSIC MAKE
WHEN TWO BAND CLASH
THROUGH ALL THESE WARS
WE CARRIED
OUR MOTHERS BASKET
PLAITED WITH ITALICISED STRAW
FOR HER RUGGED HARVEST
OF RED KOOLAID
AND BAKED CHICKEN
THIGHS
ELEGIAC
PRESSED AGAINST
POEMS IN THIS NERVOUS
CENTRE

PULLED   SHE
        OUR SMALL HANDS
    AND SPLINTERS
        WHERE THE WEIGHT
    CUT
        HER SHOULDER
                TO FRAGMENTS
WHEN A BOTTLE SMASH
        AND THE BAND GET SLACK
AN SCATTER
        OUR LAUGHTER SWUNG
    FROM DEEP MAGENTA HAZE
            SOME WOUND THERE
        HER BREAST STILL
                        SORE STILL

THESE WIRES
        BENT INTO PURPLE TIARAS
AND GUINEA FISHERMAN POLES
        FLAGS AND THEIR EMBLEMS
            WHICH SHOOK ROME
OF ITS SILVER
    WITH DREAD
        BEARDS OF MUD
    FROM CREATION
        AND DISSONANCE OF
            MUD
BLACK BENIN TOPSOIL
OF EARTH
            MOIST WORD
        OF THE GRIOT
COME HIS COME

CHANTING
    FROM SOME HOUSE OF DIN
        WE ABSAILED FROM
TO FIND HIM
  IN A DUSTY FIELD
    STUTTERING
      IN RAY MINOR

    — SANS HUMANITÈ —

    CHARLOTTE STREET AND DUKE STREET
  CORNER
SIMPLE SO WE SUCK SUGARCANE
    WATCHING MAS
BUT ALL THIS TEMPORAL TILL
  WEDNESDAYS ASH
    WE THERE
  SATYR TAILED
AT GREEN CORNER
  WE WAS
  BULLET HOT BY ROXY ROUNDABOUT
  WE WAS
  CHIPPIN FOOT AN SHUFFLIN
    LIKE PARADIDDLE
RIMSHOT
  LIKE GALVANISE
    FROM HURRICANE
  WE THERE
AT GREEN CORNER
    WHEN MACHETE PELT
      AND THE ROAD GET RED
    FROM ALL THAT

SUPER 8

SATURATES

AT ARIAPITA AVENUE
ADAM SMITH SQUARE
QUEENS PARK WEST AND CIPRIANI BOULEVARD
WHERE THE ASPHALT BLINKS
WITH DECALS STREWN FROM
SEQUINED QUEENS
PIXELATED IN
THE ST ANNS AIR
UNDER THE
ALMOND TREES
AT MEMORIAL SQUARE
WE WERE
FLESH IN THE SWELTER OF
TROPIC FRUIT
SOAKED
BRINEWAYS
FIRE
AND THE LASH OF IT
WAS A HUMMINGBIRD
COAST WE SAILED TO
A MASKED BALL
WE INHERITED
MASKS WE STOLE
MANSIONS WE OVERTURNED IN

SO SHALLOW IS THIS
MEMORY THAT IT PIERCED ME LIKE
CHIRICAHUAN ARROWHEAD
CEREOUS
DROWNED IT IN DOUBLE

BEATEN GOATSKIN DRUMS
FROM GUST AND PLYWOOD
    JUNCTIONS
WHERE BLISS THROAT SPARKLES
THERE
    EVEN
LIKE SEA SILT AND
        JETTY FISH
NEAR PORT AUTHORITY WHERE
        CRUSIE SHIPS LANDED LIKE
    SPACESHIPS TO THIS
DREAMSCAPE

    CONTEMPLATING
    THE ROAD

OUR
    VERGE OF MEMORY
        SPLIT LIKE CANE WITH
CANBOULAY FIRE
    WITH GILPIN
TO PLANASS // LEFT MARKS FROM
        FLAT SIDE OF THE BLADE
AND MY GRANDMOTHER
    SAID HOW STEELBANDS
        USED TO CLASH
        THERE
IN THAT SACRED PLACE
NEAR BELMONT VALLEY ROAD
    SO DARK WOULD NEVER
        CATCH HER
          IN PORT OF SPAIN

WE SAW THE WEBBED WINGS OF THE CARNIVAL
    QUEEN
                ISIS FLUTTERING
    IN HER SECOND SKIN
        PEEP
HER HALO
    AND THE UNDERLUNGS
        OF HER SADNESS
AND THE SEQUINED SPICE OF HER
    PERSPIRING
CAPTURED BY BLUE BOX FLASH TUBE
    TELEFUSION AND DIFFUSE RELAY
        THESE IMAGES
    THE CLACK CALACKA CLACK OF
            THE MIDNIGHT ROBBERS
        COLLECTION BOX
                AND HIS TALL BLACK
    OVERCOAT WITH STARS AND
        SKULLS AND SMOKE
    BLACK/SKIN
                GLISTENING WHITE
                    WITH PAINT

AND DEEP SIGNAL
    RED
        FRESH PAINT SCENT
SENT ALONG THE AVENUES
    WAS WHEN WE KNEW
        CARNIVAL WAS COMING
SO POLAROID ON THIS HOT ROAD
                WITH TALL
STEMS OF THE JUMBIE
    RODE STILTS TO

```
              CROSS                    BACK
       OVER                     OCEANS
           AND OVER FROM
                   SHACK TO STAGE
           PERCHED ON
           BARBED WIRE
— SPEW AND REVOLUTION —
           AND THE COSQUELLE AND
               THE DAME LORRAINE
LIFTING HER DRESS
       WAS SATURNALIA


WE      CARRIED HIM
           THE KING
COLLAPSED UPON
           OUR SHOULDERS
       HE WORE WINGS
BENT FROM MONGOOSE BONE
       HEADPIECE OF GOLD
           RADIATING
FROM PERSIAN GOLDMINES
           ROAD MAKE TO WALK
SO WE CARRIED HIM
               TOWARDS ST JAMES
IN THIS BLUE DEVIL LEAP
               NOTHING
       IS SACRED
               EXCEPT HIS TUNIC OF ABSTRACT
SILK AND MOLLUSC


— MUSCLE IN THE AIR —
       TO ABASIA
```

WAS MILES
WE WALKED
WITHOUT KNOWING
AND EACH STREET THE NEXT
TO SATURATE
THE BLISS OF IT
OPAQUE STEEP
WITH BOUGAINVILLEA
& SUPER 8
RED

Blues for Cousin Alvin

Many yards had frizzle-neck fowl
and sheep as white as country cotton.
Baby geese in wire pens   on one side
of the road, bungalows.

My Humber cycle was parked one side,
and on the other side/a forest grew —
of giant hog plum trees, papaya fields
all between : the bungalows.

Hillside of Malick village
    and I am leaning
on a pillar post spitting
        Banana seeds
when cousin Alvin come dancing up from the bottom of the bush
to say some thief stook from bike to spoke,
    from chain and wheel tout bagai!

So a run down in de neighbour yard
an a grab dey 3canal cutlass.
     Was go a was goin down de gulley
       in dey mudda arse.
   Till Alvin say 'Better jus
       lower dat blade oui,
         cause dem boys don't play
         down in the bungalows.'

O he lived in the holy mud

where my real folk blues was.
O he lived in a plywood house
with paraffin angles and
     sea cockroach
         runnin bout.

And as we stand there on the jungle wall
  we see a ship pull the horizon

————shut————

Jack Spaniard nest
        wrap up under galvanise
                Cross cut teak appropriate
    to this weather
A horner man beeps — fish man — fish hand
                with scales
plastic flowers and the pink thick drapes

All these hills are home. All these cliffs and holy
        mountainsides.
Holding on to my people and my people holding onto me and
sudden so the rain came brewing down hard on the hills of mists
of ghosts across the hillsides coming down on these shacks on
these hills my mother suffered in hills of ghosts across the mists
of hillsides coming down and the ocean calling me : away from
the rayo valleys
                and the all night gospel radio

My sister with the sling of love
My sister with banana bread
My sister with the ketch-ass-shack
what breaking down
My sister with the horner man
My sister with the kente cloth
My sister with the tenure track
My sister with the muddy gust of tears

And our mother
        who art in heaven

for Amryl, Avion, Makedia and Martina

with the acolytes and wooden crosses
coming up Jitman Drive
in the stinginstinging rain

Curtis

When I see Curtis last August
that yellowbone day after the rain in Five Rivers,
leaning against his blue bottom door
an he show me he sore foot how it ban' up.
An he say how it pain him like hell, and he creak the hinge
so ah peep how the bandage was leaking.
An how foot fly does zoot there so
in his earthen room — linoleum and smoke —
I never did know — that 2 month later I be getting this
  message
   in winter
When breeze have teeth.
And it choke me right here so an a couldn't even bring
one word to speak.

In New Street, Tunapuna, by the ravine,
Curtis say 'Fellas, leh we go an get some dead'.
Them days 'dead' was in chicken fried.
And we walk all up Indian farmland.
But was take Curtis take we to some backyard slaughtery
and buy up a few bag a frozen fowl.
And he laugh like echo chamber.

Wood lice was rot from his room that August day.
And burnt milk was blowing from his pitch oil stove.
And I wondered then, 'But you foot, mister man,
  like it weeping black rain? An when sorefoot bleedin so
  it doh heal.'

And when I get the news   I put on my winter coat
     and went out into the night   to teach.

Cutlass

When de cutlass flash
de cutlass can cleanse
can cutlass can clear bush
can cutlass clenched

till sparks grew from stars fallin
scrapin the road
on jouvay mornin
Or cut can lash
a man's bare throat
cut from runnin sideways fastest
from brutal blade work
It make him run out of his shadow
make him run out of his skin
make him run out with a tumblin blade
he pulled   sharp across his throat   till it brittle
an he gullet spew
to irrigate the village vinery

was the same cutlass that slit the pig throat
like a razor
an the body shook
Hang it up and let it drip its oil and ambergris umber
Let oil run all down this holy tributary
where the corn stalks keep snakes
and wildflowers
Let it run all long the bamboo track
that leads to the Valencia river
where Sister Phyllis is weepin prayers in glossolalia
and inscribing a vever for Legba

And an old man is cutting sheaves of sage
            scythe ways or Sundays
cleaving coconuts with a three-canal blade
        And the nut well bleed
                        and it humble
            cutlass when it flash
            an it cut his achilles

        The same cutlass swung from my brother's hip
when we went hunting up Kandahar hill
        for sacred reeds and flute wood
        naked as we born in this blooming heat
            up Five Rivers jungle

Was cut that lash the horsewhip snake in two
        against the orange tree
                    make we strip it twist and pour hot oil
                    in its living wound

O ma Sylvia
your spirit vest still with me it still with me
your trance of sorrow still
dry and heavy

and the crying bird of your throat
is a hummingbird
for you are loa of birds

Once I was cutting feet for wooden men
        shaping their bones on the steel
                    and somehow snapt the blade's hot handle
                    and saw the grinning edge rise up

and strike you
            central in the temple
O ma Sylvia
                with the hilt

        you was washing white sheets
                        in the side house sink

Santa Cruz

In Santa Cruz, the bush, the insect nests and growth
on the branches and the calabash root.
The maldjo ash an sap that oozed
    from the plum tree trunk
        so slack and clear.

I climbed the Chenet, the Sapodilla
and the Dudus mango tree
        with white lice on its leaves.
Paraplegic fruit ruined to rot in that epic of mandrake
        behind the pig pen
where the bush was serpent fresh
and the earth stayed wet
under riverless bridges and the talcum fog
        of Pipiol village.

Long grass grew in the gardens of Ignacio and Tanty Margaret.
While they sat sippin cocoa tea in their tapia bungalow,
reaming through rolls of old photographs
for maps of Orinoco.

Attached to South America
        by the fingertips.

The Bamboo Saxophone

BELL

This spark arcs a sediment,
    describes a fluent form.
                (her halo broke)
                (her engine froze)
I ply
    shutters loose, make my fist my horn.
        Blow // till my spitty sound rose and tumbled
and my sleeping eye flickered
    in the hologram — dream/
        I blinked to change the scene.
                (Her fever rolled)
                (Her slack wound sewn)

REED

Once from the spacecraft where we slept on,
    broken bare by our journey,
        and the old wooden engine
went grinding through island countryside.
And I walked behind my father, watching
                the scope of his back.
        In a rigid hand   he holds
        an ox horn trombone.

BARREL

My brother and I, we in jungle now.

We roam through country for sacred bamboo
        — thick/tapered,
brown and wet, the bell end was full up
        with buds of fungus and ringworm.

The other end to blow
        was a soft seam of black crapaud truffle.
I took a stick and said 'Back off this!'
        And lumps of old tar balm and gutty oil,
                bits of wood liver — a little blood came out —
        when I poke it under.
                All these things kept the sound hid,
                        sealed
                        and holy.

The wind gauge made true scale
    but I preferred a reed,
        a fipple reed, a reed that would rattle and so
                we kept on.

Carenage

Just a glimpse
                                    of sky

        driving along the coast
        to Carenage.

The surf blinkt between fisherman huts.
                crooked wood. the land tilt
from the steady tug
                of sea beneath.

Magga dog run undulating yards.

        — blue —
        — the blue salt of sky and St Peters fish
            rockin' in the splash.
The nets they've hung
            from palm to sapodilla
are curtains that sway to reveal
                the blushing gust
                            of the sea.

The wet salted scent
        of my brother's back
            at Carenage with its pebble bay.
        Just a poor man's beach that take bus to reach.
    No deep breath
                over lush valleys.
    No grinning bliss of sand.

No lookout over fables of cocoa.
No shark an bake shop. No palms.

Bus ride through the fisheries —
                    fruit shack an pavement.
Bus ride over precipice —
                    rock stone girdle brace.
Bus ride past the bauxite factory —
           army treasury,
                Hart's Cut Bay.

And tonight I call my brother
    from a room of sighs
still missing the sea

        .infinitely

The Regal

At Regal cinema by the San Juan abattoir we meet.
In the market square with the pale scent
of cow foot fish and rotting fruit
and the slippery alley black with such blood.
Backroads of the red dusk, terracotta
in its high grim cruciform of tropic Alamo.
And the looming precipice of its heathen spire
smoked with subtitled Corbuccis.
No reels rattled here since my mother used to steal away
to watch westerns on its drapery,
years before this copper sun we meet
when she brings me her sad secret.
How she felt the earth shiver in her bosom,
left side of her breast like an arrow.

APERITIVO in CONCERTO
ritmi del nostro tempo

DOMENICA 24 NOVEMBRE 2013 ore 11.00

ROUTE
JAZZ AROUND THE WORLD

ANTHONY JOSEPH
& THE SPASM BAND

www.aperitivoinconcerto.com

MEDIASET   PUBLITALIA '80

Rubber Orchestras

2011

Heritage

for Earl Lovelace

Long before the feast days of Cairo,
the local branches of the ivory bourgeoisie
were progressing through the jungles of colonialism.
There, at night, on the surface of the physical plane,
African culture existed
without motive or decisive conflict.
Mineral strata of its power to simplify. The wood
of the north weighed heavy on the river.
But the native was disturbed.
His people spoke of rivers
and yet their revolution
was of grip and jungle,
degrees of monument
sketched out in combat and fire.

I have not spoken of
these ceremonies of image,
anticipation
of the visual agilities
of several echoes,
the black walnut trees
nor the black and gold grapes of critical spirit
nor mirrors of impassable green shadows
tearing petals from the corolla,
away from its starway and balcony,
swung out from gateways of orthodox priests
with barriers of sacred texts.

Starting from these seamless continuities
where negritude stood,
fraught, poetic and deeply human
yet entering through divination
and geographical theatre
into the centre of some corporeal potency
where nature was hidden
in jaw bones and flowers.

In the African past
the image is full of colour
and three times as long at its peak.

Dimanche Gras

I started off as a dancer,
in terms of democratic suffocation
    and that
is the way it was. At that time
in the status arenas of calypso style
consummate calypsonians hid delusions
of arenas. I went to San Fernando
in my formative years,
learnt amazing
microphone tricks. And that
is the way it was.
But in twenty years I made no money from calypso
despite controversial and rigorous customs,
blue and super in absurd quarries of water and gutter,
even living in pan maker land
left by elders to sacrifice
depths of temper and struggle —
for calypso?

That was in 1975
when the ideology of spiritual commerce
was lewd and calculated, darker and more resilient.
There were calypsonians, for instance,
who drove down to Mayaro expecting beach and resort.
Who sat in the audience
with ambition and brand.
Who sold truckloads of beer
in the night clubs of Berbice, Guyana
while steelbands clashed and the chorus line was 'War!'

The evolution of brass and divine syncopation is Ed Watson.
Mano Marcelin in Brooklyn.
Garfield Blackman, both Afro and Trinidadian.
Black like Black
        Stalin and Shadow. I go down there again
by Jogie Road Saw Mill
and see Europe kissing calypsonians on the neck.
Rudder, Aloes and Cro-Cro — dem is man!
I go down there again, got married twice,
        got written down.

Sonnet

Every thick lip said hot prayers
in my father's house.
His body in a basket, his blue alleys
were secrets which fell without volition
onto the space above his tortured mouth.
The women said nothing.
They came, sheltered in the well of hours.
But my father's beard was broken
in the covetous pulse of mirrors.
Dust pain in his dialect sent
for rocks of clean milk.

Rhinoceri

for Sascha Akhtar

Breathlessly
      she bent down
to geographical maps and cybernetic machines.
In a liturgical envelope
      of silence
she came to rest: rhinoceros,
slate tiles (hypercubicas)
with the insoluble ugliness of atavistic simulacra.

Coccyx and the inner ear, precise as oxidised silver.
Precise as Karl Marx on Huntington Hartford Bridge.
Hyper-almond or the nymph (that stalks) Joan Miró.
Visceral, like surrealist dream-death in Paris,
or revolutionary dramas that ran back and forth
with mathematical focus between
the liturgical and ascetic. She is irrational and clings
to my mouth (my mouth) in geometric rhythm,
swollen and intransigent, sensual but meticulous
and undoes the nuclear mystic.

Each function of spiral, of neck, of infinite and original
      rhinoceri
is marvellous, savage, terrestrial and supremely beautyfull.
Inlaid with ivory and paranoid rocks of the Mediterranean.
I am looking for its bronze teeth
in the mouth of the jungle, beneath
oblique precipes and hill tracks.
      Rhinoceri
(as opposed to abstract)

Red Dragon Band

In 1930 Decca hit white New York with the half-tone calypso
and creole Belairs were thrown to evil men in Harlem.
The best orchestra was the Red Dragon Band
from Hell Yard. They emancipated the biscuit drum, the brake
drum, the spoon. They were overheard at the Village Vanguard
and Carnegie Hall — flung against the uproar
of empire and rhyme.
Red Dragon Band in this conquered land
put riot in the teeth and in the Antilles
with grace in dance like masquerade bands.
Dry River Devil is the contra dance, the reel.
Red Dragon Band was a downtown thing.
Stick men hid the chorus under tarpaulin.

Présence Africaine

Joans's velvet
        landscape
disorients
        shadows
expresses its form
        as electrical forests

Cesaire's
        virgin
of presence
   promises
        metamorphosis
initiates
        itinerant   parades
becoming
            engines of cease
            -less and fugitive

        transparence

engines of Egypt and surprise

Speak the Name

it is good to promise but not
to the deep fallen brown
of sadness in the flute wind

good to bird calls and to priests
from a forest fresh with rind
and the bamboo's eye

good to the bamboo root
that reaches the jewel heart of fear
and the precious trees of El Tucuche

if you are wise
and rich with a choir of timber
birds may whistle in your temptation

speak the name
   which can break
      the fighting cock's back

from the hollow river where I used to live
in august
with the furniture
of a schoolhouse
      perpendicular
      like a landslide
where the bird rested on its back
like a memory
philharmonic in the ghost bush

where the rain fell near the candle bird's nest
like a hymn swung from a trembling throat
    harmolodic
in the ghost bush
like cocoa frogs in the elbows of the land
and the fine grey scent from the fermentary
was like a letter sent
      from a wooden book of dreams

Capybara

Cool and dead like long brown shoes in an Akashic coffin.
Rimmed like a nation of Baptist promises and desirable bells.
With sapphire skin, thin skin of night.
Who hurried back to San Juan?
Whose right side of hip belonged to pleasure?
Who came
        shuddering
in the dining room
on a black leather chair
deep in athletic water?
Who humming birds
in black pitch bush
died alone in the house of the Capybara?

        And Trinidad,
pinpricked with departments
at The Ministry of Light,
push those waves of fizzing foam from your throat.
Your sister waits in those Hindu hills.
Her laugh, and see her airport uniform,
nestled in the footfall of that nauseous heaven
like dust on the roof of time.
Every subtle twitch, her very intention
remained in the church.
But the Deacon brewed the turbulence
of an ill fitting Jesus. In Port of Spain
the cold Capybara's brain is lifted up and eaten.

Its eyes still flash.
Venetian red in the latitude
of these cruel trees.

I fall in love
too easily.

To Paint is to Wound

My surrealist friends from Portlligat,
I have come with infinite dreams
of Rhinoceri horns at the Louvre,
the less naked coccyx of the lacemaker
from the dirty cities of the Mediterranean
where everything converges like an erotic portrait.
I cannot bear
the swollen belly, the oxidised mascara,
the Naples yellow of the olive leaf,
the lithographs of Madrid, splattered with butterflies.

In November, touching the canvas with hibiscus, efficaciously
as it was, with geographical maps of the champagne rooms
of Los Angeles.
Its biological shadow
long since forgotten from scientific fantasy
yet prodigiously stimulated between thumb and waistcoat.
I promised myself
orations in Latin sent by teletype,
to paint the vitreous magic of the skull splitting.
Murmur my name
like a cauliflower
or a soft boiled egg. The devil himself
and the aesthetics of fire,
before I have advance of Spain,
I begin.
To carry the carcass to its audience in Italy,
to gnash my teeth on wheelbarrows
in which I have brought the banal
from the hills of Montserrat.

Blue Hues

She said blue — like a strange heel
steps out of bed
hunting with devilish technique
— trick bag in her hand —
the river forest hid a palace
recap of the blue slash and pocket
we walked sliver of a deep
her confection was flame-red
like bursting inside —
exquisite and parted her lips
      cheek bones of her
beat back the black hustler
drag played the con for sure
like old crow whiskey
in the Swedish bosom of her lullabye

Her hairy thighs quivered
side of the bed
blue like fifteen echoes of winter
southbound to boulevards of dirty kickbacks
weeping like Ma Rainey
with her speckled head she guaranteed
a fifty-fifty split
there was a funk box in the rocking room
and I was years well heeled
So I played a tight con
in the hard eyed world of big time crooks
Once the half witch crushed blood in my rainstorm
and awfully in love

I wore a beige bucket hat like a jitney driver
starving in a bargain for coins and Dutch head
with a broken shinbone
dope racket slick and mean
like some hurting thing
till the leather tong snapped and sealed
the sweet miracle of her breath and hip
blue blowoff in the slum section
built upstairs
of gorilla pussy and champagne

SIDE B

I decided on brown-skinned broads with poisonous bodies
throbbing in the aisles of Blue Lester Boulevard
Folks came bringing red jelly in jars
to the con mobs stationed there
I sighed with a honey bouquet
that Sunday in the riddle lands of Illinois Jacquet
Rigged on a winner with a blossom of thighs

I followed her beneath the wash-basin
where she hid bullets from the whip shop
Discarded like a sawbuck jaw — smoked grey
with prison atmosphere
Kidneys in the brown sockets of cush and nigra musk
her goddess ghost roost but I was drinking
telescoping tonic from the top coat of a trick
who played a gypsy violin
and reached the ring of something stitched
by country grifters

Bullet in the hotter rocks
Drum cuff on the sidewalk and probably Pearl
She was on the phone drawing deep breaths
while I turned dapper and pawned
snarled and rabid from the neck
at the yellow skinned girl
Like a solid citizen
of the split-cut double-saw con

Bloodstained in the hallways
with chrome in the kink of punk
I imploded at the train station
slick and elegant as a snake
and veined with terrible guts

In Baptist Distances

Made of metal but no longer sinful
in the pension-white north,
I came to Memphis through a rough door,
head to my feet in the sunshine frame
of scripture and tangible heritage;
black in the triangle, was worn as wood
in the church of swollen winds.
We heard that Bob, in medical school
found a cheap scar.
Rinse out his mouth for a black imp, paralysis
in his blood and study of life.

I shot hard marbles, made devils' work
in the puzzle rooms of St Lucille's Spiritual Temple.
The creole sickle was offset
in the vertical image of the eldest child.
And Mother Nixon, perilous
in the bamboo colonies,
and Mother Brenda, again,
illuminated with delicious scents
at the French country market, fell asleep
with a parable in her lap.

Fire Music

Jazz is a bone in a village of percussion,
spirit duality and Latin intention,
a river of vigorous spirits
with the curtain drawn back.

The season of prayer that Trane suggested
was the new thing. But the impulse
to bypass the modern and implicit
was Mingus
in ¾ time
      and in Shepp
       — the verbiage.

Two Inch Limbo

Snail messengers
from tobacco gardens
bring thunder to the land of the south
      Legba
in his palanquin
      with ten thousand earthquakes
and a plague of ants
      with the drum of moon
and Ethiopian harps
      with the grace of grass cloth
and baobab fibre
      — Orchilla —
sees the leopard in the drum texts
      and eyes
in the Euphorbia tree.

Griot

for Keziah Jones

Symbolic of the fruit of creation
whose impure sound
is the sound of universal culture,
of vocal music of black Africa,
blown into the mouthpiece with
imaginable notions
of transverse ivory trumpets.
Not to mention
this harp
which everyone can play.
The bow is a curved stick,
the bowed fiddle, earth bow
and the diffusion of pitch and pluck
is like the buzzing comb
seated in the python's womb.

Release. From bondage of god and beauty
to the sky rhythm
of superhuman choreography
and the intonation of syllables
within skinned instruments
and the vernacular languages of the Nile Delta.
Oh harp, the epic string,
the Griot's art is in listening.
The drum stick strikes the voice with memory
like the legendary horns in the orchestras of Gabon,
in the operas of vertical Nigeria

where the slit-drum speaks its prayer of timbres
each echo is a receptacle of traditional sound,
earth-bow, calabash, crocodile,
      stone.

The five stringed harp is stretched to encircle
the ear and the flesh of air
and the jingling bells
worn around the neck
and the mouth-box of the Griot
with its riddles and spells.
The bata drum is virtually a heel,
magnetic tape cannot hold you
      : sky god
of stone and sonorous wood.

The Reverend

The Reverend went down
to American residential units.
He expressed himself in some old factory
between Askaris and bicycles.
He delivered his sermons with firmness
and gestured towards
several teenage mothers
who never spent summers
in Roseland, Illinois.
The Reverend turned towards the magnifying glass
with its crystal set in poor soil.
He praised its geography, its dark visitations.

Your father slept beside the central river.
His apparent direction is Swahili.
His true vine is holiness.

Haiti

Severe and inspired by West Indian tribal tongues
which colour our judgement of neglected humanities.
My creoleness in the garden city of old world realism
of skyscrapers and deities, of image and lung.

The slack mask of an icon crushed into conquest,
by political faith and magic, philosophical myth
and regimes of trickster gods, puppetries of theatre
and rainbow alchemies of space,
defeated by intensity and intricate heart and light.

This form of allegory is my Caribbean.
Space prisons far flung
from drowned landscapes,
great forests, dream body of marble
orchestration of soul and echo
trampled in the bias of fear.

Each image
dead as in
permanent,
complete and minimal,
intuitive strata of place and self. The southerner confesses,
suffers violence, decay,
and the unconscious weight of psyche and sea.
Extreme. It is a symphony
of Marxist dialect and West African peasantry,
this tribal world of social fiction,
the passive voice of your shadow,
in layers of sound and gesture.

From San Fernando with a face like fiction,
from the admiral to the island, to the animal's tribal past.
Unfinished in New York, fossil, bone,
garment upon garment, native, for generations to come.
     Haiti,
I add epitaphs of music
to your heartland of rainforests
and impossible rivers.

Woodbrook

During the decades of King Solomon
there were dragons and Yoruba horn sections in St James.
The police maintained the bamboo territories
with gramophone organs and copious blood.
The Venezuelan army was equally ribald
and had devils in the brass band,
boot black in the Marine Gazette.

The fish market in Arouca hid stickmen from vagabond vernaculars
who snake-danced into daybreak at the Skin and Fly.
And in the creole ballrooms
stilt walkers wore short skirts.
The chantwell sang for the Royal Dutch line
and on a chair to the rear of the Sovereign Union
an orchestra from Curacao played a Spanish waltz.
Other islands knew electric light and waterman jubilees
but in Woodbrook we wore no masks
from Gold Coast to prison van.

Philly's Congo Prayer

Philly Joe released a heavy schedule
of insistent space
steaming
   overbearing
then on the second night,
Jones and his fellow Philadelphians came
from Monterey
with saxophones and an organist
who worked full time at the Middle Eastern Village
and played blue changes
        ferociously
in rhythms between
African careers and quartets
which played conventional Jazz.

That autumn Tyner left
and went searching
for hidden improvisations,
spiritual blues
and sentimental identification
within a higher plane.
Trane drove down to New York
but Trane was only the vehicle.
Trane himself said
        — Miles,
sat there five, six
sextet tracks
with Jimmy Cobb and Don Byas.
Bebop creation and the black pearls.

        Tenor sight.
    Congo blues.
            Leaning,
as in gospel.

Dolphy died tragically
but he still had 20 bars to blow.
Accented on the eight beat,
nervous like arpeggios.
His security of tone, his intervals.
Trane
played hard along the thin edge of false fingering
with the dorian scale
and a thumb piano
he bought in Stockholm.

Poem for Franklin Rosemont

Beyond words or destinations,
visual and multiplying,
intricate and persistent,
they found a faraway place in Paris.
Its potential splendour hid sequels and contrary sex
in the early hours of 1960.
Proclivities of struggle and synthesis
within the most complete utopia
of fire and speed.
Dream letters were drowned in invisible stars.
Silent suburbs of Jazz and primitive hell
were spontaneously glimpsed
in rigid cities in which
these souvenirs were read
at the Chicago Public Library
    shuddering
        loosely
on the avenue between
Greene and Zion.

These are the definitions of the palace of signs.
These are the masks with which
I hitchhiked across the wonderland
and travelled by radio to resemble that mask,
eccentric and boundless
in the image of you.
Past stairs and doorways,
past Afro-American ruins,
bamboo by the dozen among those denizens of marvellous film.

Dead
yet actually distant. Exhilarating
like dissident blues swung from the Zydeco
to the brutal suburbs of Pharaoh Sanders.
Emerging from light
into some literary response.

Angela

Her digs east were different from mine.
Mischief in her taciturn boots.
She got to the new music and dug
graves under that wooden shack.
Dirt there be rich brown like police milk.
Long punk and hired in the five boroughs.
Serious like sacrifice, she kept slimline,
dyed deep black in the orgies of Memphis.

I spent the evening at the airport jail
and then I heard the sorrow songs of the South.
Dub door in hook and cochineal thrones.
I never saw Angela yet I knew her.
I knew the mist in the eye of her root and rice.
How she tumbled down like country blues
from her wooden bed, in her bebop robe.
She could crack a needle with her lock jaw bone.

Audrey

Impressions of my mother's house
lashed by lean and physically elegant
hydraulics. The sugar crop now, the bauxite,
I mean — Audrey, bathed in the landscape on both occasions.

I sat near the station in Suriname;
fabric of a republic, the poet among the flood,
high from a sighing radio tree — Audrey, I mean,
bathed in light on two occasions.

Nations

Poetry dominates meaning

GASTON BACHELARD, *The Poetics of Space*

An edifice in a web of darkness,
becomes insignificant.
Its green leagues devoted to trees.

Such a house, a tower,
immense with the densest fluid,
considerable, an implicit geometry.

A paradox at close range,
geography, supernatural in the ramparts,
a village of lizards and architects.

A poem: speak it,
the cosmos moulds it
and trembles with silence.

A dovecote in a daydream, with starways,
askew in the dead tree.
It is the seed.

Nothing transmits its aromatic salt.
Its empires are dust.
Terrestrial objects of the heart.

A Ditch of Knives

To be national, liberty is impossible.
Nothing but the rotting rape of the aboriginal circle.
The struggle is self saddled with spiritual poverty
and the chief dignitaries are incapable of fiction or charity.
Idyllic in the slight camp with the vigorous style of militant men
deep in the cult of Africa.

The vultures raid the muscle
to a harvest of meat.

This is the woman who rebels.
This is her strength, her air and agony.
She explodes in the countryside — fetish of her private regions,
minerals of her cunt, her energies and grip on fact.
She may be a desert nation, the living expression
of terrifying fruit. But hell is the hostile world of hard men,
perverse and colonial like a ditch of knives.

Lester Young

The whales and the fish
  circle back from tenderness
 to Memphis
  to where Lester leaps in
  to the apparition of Jazz
   and physical chanting
of the black
 blues
  breath of the body is
 blues
  black roots and alcoholic sutras
  of dreaming
 in articulate and spontaneous transmission
 of stanza
 and margin

Riff For Morton

Damper down —
        both phallic and acquainted
with African blues.
        The hips suggest
hot Jazz.

The African fiction of whiteness is absolute.
Arcade saloons and dance halls,
gambling down like evil or false notes,
blue notes of white magic.

Jelly Roll Morton
        at the Cadillac cafe,
pimp or piano drunk and sick
on the bricktops of Vancouver.

Ragtime Billy
        from Chicago
a clarinetist at the Regent went southwest
with the wrath of Poseidon gambling down
in terrific storms which broke down
the Pensacola kid at the Paradise Gardens
with the first three notes of 'Dead Man Blues'.

Morton left diamonds
and cash on Cadillac cars.
Duke Ellington had swing bands,
Basie and Calloway had a cluster of tricks,
which in fact were spikes at kingpin sessions.

And in the exact rooms of the Kidworth Hotel
where days passed like clinic cards,
Morton left the Sepia Spot and took his body to the Jungle
    Inn
on 126th North West
where restless priests listened to Pops Mabel
at the church of intercourse.

Yes he left Mamanita.
Yes he let his beard grow.
Straight down to the bottom,
he's spittin blood in the broom closet.

Jelly you rascal you minstrel you lover you
bone meat of the creole Caribbean
— vicious semen, Jelly,
bake 'em brown and break a banjo across their backs.
Jelly you blues talker you, the voodoo of your laughter,
stepping lean in stove pipe suits, down
        to the very end.

In Vibrant Oases

In vibrant oases called Davis
I hear this.
His big sad eyes reflect
dark Latin hats, berets.

The big band swings
and Slim sits down.
He put them to move
and carry on —
but mostly — I had the luck.

So we danced around
with a sobbing blues,
then we went up river
to get our names back.

Sonnets for Albert

2022

light

Light, fill the air around these houses.
May my grandmother continue to water her roses
and touch the aloe fronds in her forever time.
Light, as you lit the morning my father arrived
unexpectedly in his new Hillman Hunter,
and Mammy ran into the yard to embrace him.
And until my grandfather put wire around the veranda

I could sit and swing my legs off the banister,
or from the garden spy up the thighs of my father's
new girlfriend, as she laughed with ankles crossed,
as Albert moulded his mother's anthuriums.
My grandmother fried fish, we ate, she was happy,
even as she knew that later that afternoon
my father would be gone again into that gone momentum.

flack and hathaway

My father would be gone.
Months into mystery.
But he persisted
in our longing.
We saw him
maybe once, maybe
twice a year. We sang
Flack and Hathaway,
that he would come running.
And while we waited
the myth of him grew,
till the anticipation
of his return
would fill each room.

jogie road

From life, from love, in shame. The red
sawmill on Jogie Road with cedar grain
in its fibrous air. Red. The old train
track and the bridge where my mother's rage
was bruising the dark. Her fingernails ripped
at my father's shirt, his face.
This is blood: the way he looks away,
then down with open palms in resignation.
But memory has a curious sting. The red sawmill
was not on Jogie Road but on Silvermill.
And in the savannah there were five saman trees
which cried when cut, not six.
My father held me over his shoulder that night.
No, I was looking up from the road.

Trinidad, 17 November 1970

a x e

My father, God bless his axe.
He grooved deep in pitch pine.
He spun his charm like bachelor galvanise
in hurricane. Once I saw him peep through
torrential rain like a saint at a killing.
And when the wind broke his cassava trees,
and the water overcame his eight-track machine,
and his clothes were swept away in the flood,
his Hail Mary fell upon a fortress of bone.
So he crossed his chest with appointed finger
and hissed a prayer in glossolalic verse.
He may grand-charge and growl but he woundeth not,
nor cursed the storm that Papa God send
to wash away the wish of him and every dream he built.

what do i know of my
father's body?

Not even a bottle of duty-free rum or a carton of Du Maurier.
This time I come with both hands swinging, arriving first
at the funeral home where you are already waiting
in your pillow box, exuding a kind of warmth.
You are my father's body. But I know so little of you.
I know the soft weight of your hands on my shoulder at the airport.
I know your rings. And I felt the muscle of your panic wrist once,
when we were far out at Maracas, and the ocean almost overcame us.
I have seen your gut grow into its own sonnet, and your head
grow gleaming and bald. But today it is your chest I come to know.
How rigid it is when I press upon the crisp sheen of your burial shirt
to thread a rose through the eye of your lapel. And I find
the pall-bearing weight of your life, when we grip the casket's chrome
to lift and carry you down to the hearse, waiting in the bright yard.

rings

I only have look at my hands to see my father.
The wide silver ring spans the proximal of my left hand's
ring finger. I remember this ring as a child, asking
my father what the raised letters spelled. But he laughed
and, like everything else made of secrets, he would not tell.
It was revealed after his funeral, when we were at the house
and the jewel bag get bring out from the bedroom
for my brother and I to choose which as heirlooms.
The bag held things which were either removed
from my father's body as he lay dying,
or kept in a saucer beside his Bible.
I chose the silver and soon deciphered that the raised letters
were his initials: AHJ, in Western typeface.
The ring fit firm and right. My brother chose a chain.

North Coast, Trinidad, 2016

el socorro

In an April of Saturdays, I visit my father in El Socorro.
He is clearly ill and living again as a bachelor. His philosophy
– that if God gives him five more years, he wants those to be happy –
has brought him here to a ground floor apartment on Jagroop Lane.

Dust in the sun beams through both rooms. The furniture is old.
Cardboard boxes of folded clothes, his tattered Bible
and pill box on the kitchen table. I take photos, saddened to see
where my father has arrived in his seventh decade.

Does my father know he is dying?

When I drive him to the pharmacy, I photograph his hands
as he flirts with the chemist's wife. What is it about his hands?
His forearm is mine, his fingers. The Saturday after he dies,
I cannot go when my stepmother asks me
to help her clear his apartment.

tina

Hear this one. The big man survey the house, he say, 'OK.
All yuh will have to break down to build back that kitchen.
While they building, them pillars could support the bedroom.
You and yuh daughter could stay in there. The living room
need new flooring, T&TEC not connecting electric
till yuh fix that roof. The wiring faulty. Fire.
Yuh talking good money: materials, cement, labour.
But Tina, yuh can't live like this – with termite, in ruins.'
He had left quite Santa Cruz to go to Five Rivers
to see what could be done for Tina and Trish.
Tina not Albert daughter, but Baptist know Baptist
and she have his last name. She dies two years after he does.
Serpent didn't possess her womb, was stomach cancer.
And two weeks after, the house she suffered to save fell down.

breakfast in dc

That night after the conference in DC, we broke free
of postcolonial tautology, to gather in the small room
of the writer in residence. We were young scholars; poets,
novelists, a journalist. We drank white wine warm and nodded
to neo-soul. I saw them recoil from the British resident when,
in the marrow dark of 3 a.m. he rightly said
that there was nothing like the sweet kick of crack cocaine.
At dawn we drove out in the doctoral candidate's car.
We saw the Doric pillars of the Lincoln Memorial
glowing in the unclear distance, then the white gasp
of the monument. We ordered pancakes with blueberries
at Pete's on 2nd Street, and shared our commonalities.
And what we shared, besides our blackness,
was that in our childhoods, our fathers had all been absent.

Santa Cruz, Trinidad, circa 2014. *Commotion, when he puts on his robe...*

the tumuli in santa cruz

Fire for you, and the mothers of the church lit candles
upon your breastbone. Fire was lit, even in the hole
to purify the earth to receive you. They poured flame
from brass goblets of croton and pink ixora.
And swung a chant to kill death:
>   *O Death, draw out your sword.*
Your body lay in the sweet brown. The red church
on the hill grew nervous in the noon. The long hearse
purred in the sloping yard. Perfume sang from the bosoms
of aunts and far cousins. Look out over mountains.
Look out where rayo trees are planted on tumuli of bones
like ladders for spirits to cross into heaven.
>   *O fold me in and fly me around the valley.*
We shall all be rooted in this well of hours, eventually.

El Socorro, Trinidad, April 2017

FILM ET CONCERT
SAMEDI 24 FÉVRIER 2018

ODE À LA CARAÏBE

CONCERT D'ANTHONY JOSEPH (UK),
PRÉCÉDÉ DU FILM *ULTIMOS DIAS EN LA HABANA*
DE FERNANDO PÉREZ

CINÉMACITYCLUB PULLY

Uncollected Poems

Jabbie, the Tailor

In Kroo Town, in Freetown,
Jabbie watched the old tailor line lapels
in his shed beside the water,
and day by day the needle and the trade
moved closer to Jabbie's hand. That pale
stub of chalk pressed shut between his fingers,
was to mark patterns and where to cut
serious cloth with scissors with jaws
      like young cutlass blades.
In the tailor's shop, where bespoke waistcoats
were stitched between steam, iron and ironing board,
the radio hung on a nail
to treble and buzz while Jabbie learned
to rim button holes by hand
      tight and
      flawlessly neat.
I found him stitching agbadas
on the Old Kent Road, as one of
two tailors working in that whirring
back room at 'Afro Design'. He was
recommended. And as he showed me
the shirts he had crafted to mannequins,
he said,
      'Don't worry Joseph, and I will make you
            something special.'
He measured my limbs, my neck, my hips
with hard fingertips from fingerless gloves.
      'And I will design you a good outfit myself,
         no pattern, no book, no scheme.

Ah hah! Now you say Fela,
      I know exactly, what you mean.
   Don't worry. From jacket to trouser
      go be fitting perfect.'
And even though it took Jabbie three weeks to stitch,
when it finish plot it suit and fit me fancy in truth,
with epaulets and pointed collars, in viisco wax green
and blue, except the trousers, which were too
exact in length — as if that were possible,
and known to be shrunk when I wore them in rain,
walking from the stage to backstage in Brittany.
I found Jabbie a month later on Peckham Rye,
he had moved to a seamstress's shop
in the covered market of Little Lagos,
and was presser-footing on his wasp waist machine,
among soon-finished dresses and scraps of fabric
shaved from gowns and wedding capes.
Jabbie, red-eyed at his engine,
took a sewing pin from his mouth,
then he stood and rubbed my shoulder and said:
      'You are my best customer.
      They jealous me here for my customers,
      they jealous me my skill, but you, but now
      you see me here, you can find me, everyday,
      but another place, maybe I somewhere else,
      I go be gone…the next day. In any case,
      I call you, when it finish stitch.'

The cloth I brought Jabbie this time was psychedelic
orange and brown, but three weeks gone
and Jabbie phone keep ringing down
      to flatline tone.

When I pass to see if my thing done sew, he say,
        'It nearly finish.'
But that man was now marking out the shirt back with chalk.
He even took my address and promised
to deliver the garment by hand that night,
that this one was different, a special design, slightly looser,
longer and fuller in the fit, the hem cut straight,
and the patterns: lining up at placket and button shaft,
was the reason why it taking so long, plus,
he also had twenty geles to stitch.
That night Jabbie never came to Camberwell,
but later next week the thing was made and fit
like he had sewn it onto my body. I had always meant
for him to build me a long red kaftan
with a Nehru collar and billowing sleeves,
something that Richie Havens might have worn
on a subway platform in old New York City, in 1969.
But Jabbie was on Rye Lane by then.
And he took me by the hand,
        'Joseph', he said, 'ask for me in the chicken shop...
and they will find me...I stop working for people now...
until I get my own shop...'
But his sunken eyes stared out
        from a deep narcotic hum,
and the rims were waxed with dirt and black sweat,
and that was the last time I saw Jabbie.

Manifesto II

Born as to become guru
of some (certain) new powerful sect
— unmistakable
in any (and every) disposition.

I do not deny, that if such
a sect emerged
it should be written down.
It is certainly < obvious >
that such a sect would lead
to any (or every) sermon
being delivered under
suspicious conditions.

A sect has its place.
Because what manages to enter
can happen during listening.
        Meaning
could transfer its image
without contumacy.

In favour of sect/definitely (or in this moment
        : whole)
and most dignified or inscribed in comments
for tomorrow.

Dubwise

I had gone to move the rain from the balcony
when sudden-so the night came in. I walked
on the outside edge behind the balustrade
was sudden death blow, I said, 'Below'.
And being written from a distance
and being so out of sync but alive
as an island that breaks away from the main,
I went into that same escarpment/encampment/apartment
where our first daughter was born.
But different.
Now, bodies filled the gap between
beat and bedroom, dancers filled the kitchen.
But there was no bass to the roots. Boo sound
humming from the living room.
Some youth had set themselves up as DJ
by moving my amp and amplitude — *boo sound* —
to install theirs. So rugged black with worn edges
overused in old blues and basement weddings —
liminal roots, blue rockers blooming into flowers
only to be scorched
by the hard air of a tower.
I get damn vex and wail upon them solid.
Leggo cuss, leggo fire. 'Who built this station,
this system, this sound? With whose machines
does the rhythm run? Who bring drum?
Who bring echo chamber to stutter over
my two three tune and radiogram?
Who entered my home and punished me
        with Sister Carol?'

— Boom and they leggo Earth, Wind and Fire
Oh 'Mr DC' —— 'In the Stone'?
I start to unplug wire one time, to plug back in mine.
But rushing to ready records to overcome theirs
kills the dance, since the dancers have to sit
on hessian rugs and wait for a mess of wires
      to unravel
           before the music starts again.

Four Shovels

1

My wife with the back of a bird fleeing vertically
   — André Breton — 'Freedom of Love'

She threw verbs and arrows at my
skull till I broke like water in her peninsula, a wife
who breathing deep, murmurs, coy-like, with
the nape of a question for a neck. The more the
heat from the galvanise slapped back
and the red dirt blew up, I thought of
how hard she suffered on that gospel plough, w/out a
suffocating word, with the exact patience of a bird
in flight, piercing the web of time, fleeing.
I broke her back with an axe of sin. To be buried, vertically.

2

all their syllables of living colour & career thru the water
   — Kamau Brathwaite — 'Dear PM'

Gust of sound and sea blast and all
the windows are rattling like teeth in their
jaws. Then the sky lid shifts to dim and syllables
of stone are chasing colour from the earth. Fear of
thunder like a child, like black dada in their roar of living.
The blood in the road below was the colour
of molasses; thick black with love &
this too, shall be the arc that frames the devil's career.
Suddenly how the junction get hot. Siren rip thru

and the sound tore straight to the
solar capital, like sorrow, leaving wounds in water.

3

fling of his wish have caught the sea
        — Kamau Brathwaite — 'Master of the Mary Jones'

Far flung from the fling
and the rip and the fever, grass in the scar red hills of
these islands. Cut across with cuss until his
imagination grew sombre. Wash under wash and wish
away from the grief of it. Fish and bug and mollusk, to have
bliss of it. The dreamscape, so tenderly caught
in the folds of terror, like a drowned man weeping in the
dark abyss of the sea.

4

In this night I moved upon the territory with combinations
        — Charles Olson — 'The Librarian'

What changes? Limestone strata in
the heat pulse of earth, the drone bee in this
tree, the firefly in the litmus of night,
terrestrial objects of the heart. I
moved   *upon the air as a leaf to dark waters*
leapt from the roof to the
plum tree, dew wet, dim was my territory.
The landscape seemed diseased, and dry with
its process of combinations.

Written from Memory

I am in the island of iguanas, of Johnny Babwah's
        'Ice Cold Coconut since 1929.'
The cart leans in the culvert, savannah side,
while the dread with the bandaged thumb
hacks my nut with his blade, and asks,
        'How long you been gone, Red Man,
        you losing your skill
        or what?'
He finds my tongue,
in a gap between language — if not all,
then plenty gone. He sell me
three mammy apple.
Remind me how to eat them:
        'Wait two or three days
        till it get soft,
        before you peel
        the skin off.'
But I have forgotten
how to keep up with a place
where everything happens at once.

Today I watched my aunt
coming down the coruscating light of the village.
Cumin scent and the water truck, the new road
like a promise still coming.
At seventy-three she takes wise steps; avoids
gulleys and thorns. She only gets to go to the beach,
she says, when I come down.

'Las' night the dog was barking so loud,' she says,
Tone, I was sure was a manicou hidin' in the calabash tree.
but when I shine the flash, only tailoring scissors, cassareep
and barb wire fall out. And that ground so blasted slippery;
every time people pass there they does piss.'

And all of this written from memory
is made more luminous with distance.
But I have lost touch with the people.
I have forgotten the heat.
        I say, 'It's getting hotter',
        they say, 'Nah, is so it always is.'
Remind me how to bear it?
        'First, let the heat out the rental car.
        Carry a rag, a change of clothes,
                carry water.'

The Inconsolable

for Kemal Mulbocus

We were eating the Mauritian biriani
your mother cooked for your sister's wedding,
while your uncles in their floppy suits,
held smiles which seemed to linger long beyond
handshakes. Wild children
unfettered the seams and ceremonies
of their wedding clothes,
to run

     between

         our heels.

Between the rice and the speeches, we hid
behind the pundit's car, to drink forbidden wine.
We bent it right from the bottle, walked the grounds.
West London sundown.
The grass was brown and pious
like the hash you crumbled
in the honest heat of your palm.

Once on Sunday we drank and watched my daughter play
in the beer garden on Coldharbour Lane. It was summer
and you said that dying was fine, but that death itself
was an inconsolable.
That no hideous key could be found
to unstitch its misery.
That any balm or philosophy was futile.
That its loop was infinite and precious
and impossible.

On that Friday, I was ironing stage wear,
listening to Donny Hathaway, *Live*, at The Bitter End.
The next day the band and I were flying to the Aegean isles.

When I entered your house,
the ground
tilted
30 degrees to the right.
I fell towards a wall.

Your wife wrung her hands in weeping
through the darkness of those rooms.

Black Summer light.

Your mother erupting
from a taxi.
Her heavy arms
flailing like windmill blades.
To fall and keep falling.
To fall and keep falling upon
the threshold of your door.

Then everything converging
like a surrealist portrait.

The Kora

After Giacometti's Woman with her Throat Cut
(Femme égorgée) 1932

We moved
through the din and dank covered market.
Warped African vinyl were dusty grooves
in floorless rooms of sacrilege. Nothing there
was worth returning with.
In the dirt lay fragments of memory, broken instruments
of ancient wood: A kora
in the dust, like
   :::: *Giacometti.*
But not twisted but black, not iron and yet
a complex science of sound
    within the wound of it.
The strings were stretched taut across the bridge
like cryptic ribs, there were knots and levers.
And when the instrument inhaled
its bowl expanded.
Unpolished bare wood and animal smell
     .Dead
Yet still breathing.

Above us
the dark hills were built from bone and rock.
Each crevice hid a home, folded flat by day.
We had walked through the desert.
Show me a stairway which has no balustrade
like steps up the neck of a sphinx,

where the edge seemed high and grinning
into a curious death. But not secret but black,
but not twisted, yet blacker.

We had taken a country drive in a leatherette heat,
deep east of the island along a squatters' path,
to a harbour of millet and vine. Blue yellow bright
on stilts and under: herbal dirt, fetish scents, secrets kept.
Memory ghost of my mother.
Memory ghost of my father
leaning against the pillar post
like it was a gleaming Ford Falcon.
His grin alone — I know — could pump energy,
it could irrigate the whole region.
                        So we kept on
            towards the ocean
Dark and deep and the boats
circling in the bay.
Road around the cliff side
                    so ruggedly steep,
took it down among the birds,
            grinning at the curve.
From down: boom and the motion twist,
something shook and bent
the air
like an earthquake — some pop a clap of thunder
in the moaning room, in the narrow valley
of the in-sta-mat-ic now —
street where we were walking
        tilting our masks,
                        eardrums we cupped
        ears, walking

to the city of mist and distance by breath,
we measured time by distance.
Country marshland. In that there far field
    the air where
    this powerful machine
    was making it lilt and linger
then
    plunge
        perpendicular
            into the soft bucolic/soul of earth —
    on impact exploding —
    a-wow-a-wow-a-look-a-dat —
close enough we saw the passengers
    : timorous and dank
    : a moment before sinking first we thought
they were dead that way they hung their heads
        but they were sitting
                in a church,
                in a hall,
                in senate
                in Houses of Parliament
                in Community Centres
                in cinemas beside abattoirs
                in Universities of Dust
                in libraries my father built
                in tents where tables are set for exorcisms
                in estival festivals
                in the hills of Montpellier
                in Never Dirty and Morvant
                in endless narcissistic prayer halls
                en divers arrondissement
                in wild Indian rivers

in civic auditoriums
in ice factories
in rooms where were made
carnival costumes
in rain lit rooms
in houses of smoke
from tall tower blocks that were burning
where they were strapped to their seats
but did not scream/when cut
but did not
    .m o a n

Aunt Pat, Bené and
the Hurricane

Sky darks above a blue river,
cattle pull for home,
pine cones clinch, candles flicker, rain:
bucket-a-drop washes hills of a village.
Some here have only gazette paper to cower under,
mud and only flags of secret colours
            to travel on upon.
There are abandoned stables, a racecourse, the high
corn blowing, the cane, the fever grass
bending in the exorcism yard
where the table rocked with leg and lumber
and the demon spoke in hideous math
to frighten people with a voice at once high pitched
and flung low like the red wounds of bush fires
still raging in the north.
            As if its voice
had never possessed a body until then.

Who has seen these ceremonies of anguish?

Uncle Bené with the bell.
Poopa Bené John
who once cast a speaking serpent
out of a woman in a ceremony
in a cane field.
Dead now, with no map home,
he stands looking out upon El Piedra Blanca,
high enough from the lash of the hurricane :::::::

locust in the swirl and sting of its tail
       above the water.
Its foam blooming against unbreachable cliffside,
wind — and a barrel capsize in the yard.
Roofs will need to be held down
by several tall men standing on tables in living rooms,
with hooks of eyes and limitless rum to be drank
from bottles shaped like bongo drummers,
grinning with bare feet and skin teeth
and billowing sleeves.

Lie.

Is Aunt Pat still alive,
barren in the bush
with the soft-candle heart?
Aunt Pat who never had children,
Pat who lived alone.
Pat who put flesh scent
in that board house,
the one with the pane-less windows,
and the cum-crusted face rags
under her bed.
You laugh? You sorrow for Pat?
You go buy galvanise when the wind blow
her house down? You go bury Pat
when she dead?

Uncle Bené shelters
from the stinging-stinging rain,
in a hut overlooking the bay.
When the sea come up

it flinging wood and bone
upon the cliff bank.
Bené want to jump
but he don't want to dead.
He know death from the pull
of high-place-phenomenon.
He know come high or come low.
He know how lighting and thunder
can't hit with one blow.
Bené maintain, to wait
in this hut where fishermen keep
their nets and oars, their hooks
and fears of drowning.
But Bené must dead.
His free paper burn.
Now he sees himself years before,
smelling his fingers, dressing
for ghetto discotheque, the one on the foreshore,
before they planted condominiums there
and it come like Miami.
Black when the red bauxite blush
still framed photos
of his brother and him,
on some Saturday,
bitter skin dry with salt,
gazing out, to see.
Wait Bené wait and the storm to pass,
the grass to fold back upright.

Aunt Pat's house is swaying in the hurricane.
        And on this night
the rain would burn a hole in the roof.

Aunt Pat pray hard, put palm to breast,
moan when she see the fisherman hut
tumble down hill and crash in squall and thunder.
Aunt Pat pray, but the roof will still fall in,
the world will end, and soon every room
will smell of lavender.
But didn't it rain? Yes, it rained.
It rained upon roads and rivers.

      O, didn't it rain?

In Istanbul

for Colin Webster

In Istanbul, there is a pomegranate vendor
outside the Grand Hotel. One arm is sober
but the other holds a blade with the point curling back
    like a scimitar.
And all this is lit by the lights of the port below,
and those on the hills above, suspended in that forever time
when the saxophonist
   is raising the horn to his mouth.
    And in that moment
      the watcher fears the reed may arrive too late —
       but it never does.

Comets

Fred D'Aguiar, Linton Kwesi Johnson, Derek Walcott
& Darcus Howe on Arena: Caribbean Nights: Poetry *(1986)*

These men is comet —
the way they pass through
       spatial time
       carve and still sculpting
       into something
       that sound like we.
These men is
       lodestar,
       midnight robber,
       calypsonian,
       promoter
       on the microphone
       chanting,
       masters of ceremony
       toasting.
       Griot with the trumpet bone
       blowing.

       Darcus mighta say:
              'Well, now we get
              to the heart-a-the-damn-thing self.
       Now we get to this intricate thing
              they call "poem".'
       These men is comet.
       Let us map the parabolae of their voices.
       But first we need language.

Mouth
   without
      language
cannot define
a halo or even a bicycle wheel.
Ear
   without
      language
cannot hear
the steel

drum!

Nor the flick between pan-stick and wrist.
   Gesture
   without
   sign
   cannot write or rewrite history.
Especially since this very
syntax aim to imprison us
unless we twist the tongue of it
and creolise the verb.
Dyam fool, you don't know the wrong poem
coulda leggo terror upon that hill
where people squatting and rebuilding their lives
word by word?
Without language
the girl child would still be bathing
on a sheet of galvanise
     in the road.

So let these four man step outta yard
and build a three stone fire.
Bubble a pot.

Each can stir it. Each can govern as each can serve.
Never mind neck tie, nor the plastic
cockroach-killer brogues
the poet from Deptford pose in.
Or the gabardine bells
ringing round the rebel poet ankle.
Or how the gentleman who fly from Boston
articulate the inner life of words
then lean back in his chair and cross his leg.
Get him vex
and he will cuss an' tumble your cathedral
with Creole that swing back from people who live near the

sea

and have to shout above the rustle
of trees … the fisheries … Castries.

LKJ coulda say —

'Caribbean poetry
is a revolutionist doctrine
occurring
when you juxtapose
uptown sound
to downbeat rhythm,
the meter, we chant down the ruler
and burn down plantation.
But strong poems still find us
between the beats.
We flash as comet in darkness.
We define what poetry is —
one beat
at a time.'

Look,
even Nello neck in a polo neck quoting Keats.
He never condescend by saying
that the sentiment of the poet remains the same.
    But in Mikey Smith, you eh find
            the twing, the twang, the tongue
                    lil' different?
Comet, you pass like a bullet
and rip up the particulars of the thing.
You rob the altar at the Abbey.
Percy Bysshe Shelley coulda jump an' say,
'In an English time, in a form of
Republican clarity.
Perspicuous in the approbation
of empirical fact and duality...'
And we woulda laugh and rim back skull an' say — 'A-A,
    a lot of these English tests
    with their bardic quest
    still tie up in implication.
    Didn't they live and benefit
    from the dreadest ruthless regime?
    Some was rebel and socialist
    who come to shell out immortal wheat.'
Mikey Smith say, 'Sure,
but they still can't speak for we.
Contemplation on the inner life
of Caribbean people
needs concentration dense
like dialect bush
and fluid like a painted river.'
The big man say, 'Yes,
but what language do you think in?'

Fred return it: 'Does thought even have language?
And if not is it not then like fine wire stretched across the yard?
Tie one end on the lime, tie the next
to the hibiscus tree, where the leaves,
fulla white lice and aphid. And upon that line,
   every doily or panty mammy hang to dry is like a feeling.
      And from this metaphor,
            when breeze blow, words come:

   ... ah ... the authenticity of bees ...
      the red pride
         of the undignified
      mango ...
      ... fruit is the song of trees ...
      ... rhythm is a unit of meaning ...'

If language is a unit of feeling
then the intellectual sensibility of my grandfather
      was decidedly poetic.
Spontaneously, he reach back from market an' say:
      'Ai boy, what time you reach home this morning?
      You take my house for some open sepulchre? Come.
      Come down in the garden, let me break a branch
      across your back.'
His poem was pitched between seduction and risk.
But the argument about whether what he utter
was a poem or not is not one Caribbean people engaging with.
The credits done roll upon authority and measure.
Trajectory of nuclei, coma and tail — these men is comet — they strike
      with force
            and blaze.

The Frequency of Magic

Poetry Performance by Anthony Joseph
23 April 2015 | 15:30h
Leselounge Fachbibliothek
Unipark Erzabt-Klotzstraße 1

Anthony Joseph is a British/ Trinidadian poet, novelist, musician and lecturer described as 'the leader of the black avant-garde in Britain'. His written work and performance occupies a space between surrealism, Jazz and the rhythms of Caribbean speech and music. He is the author of four poetry collections and a novel The African Origins of UFOs. In 2005 he was honoured by the Arts Council of England and Renaissance One as one of 50 Black and Asian writers who have made major contributions to contemporary British literature.

Don't miss this rare opportunity to see the legendary poet and performer live!

Selected Lyrics

Robberman

From Bird Head Man *(2009)*

— Hide the obeah you bring for me —

Robber man don't get me
      don't blow me down
           town
                down shantytown ravine
where they beat silver fish an' wabeen
      on the riverbank.

We come like ripe guava
when it season
      full it ripe
           an sling it shot like a 12 gauge shot
                that shatter the wings of our mountain gods.

The young blood seep up on the sea an float foam.
An he reel so reel that the paddle broke
    and he tumble down
      cliff an crocus bound.
          Better just hide the magic for me.

Robber boy
Don't make mud clog the tracks I cross riverbank.
Don't sell my eyes for sand puppet teeth.
Don't seed my seppy for ransom.
Don't brug my neck with fisherman's twine.
Don't scope my ruse with barbed river time.

Don't fix my suffer with jumbie symposium.
Don't grief my root with rumours of wounds!
                    Come on
                    an just
                    hide
                    the magic
                    for me.
Hide the magic for me.
comecomecomecomecomecomecomecome
Leh we pounce on wild Quenk an Agouti,
like we used to.
                    Make we shuffle in the jungles
                    of Port of Spain.
                    Leh we stop
                    all this war an' ting
                    Leh we lime.
                    like we used to.
                    leh we love.

Time: Archeology

From Time *(2014)*

If a father kills his own son in self defence
then sets the bones in a calabash gourd,
the bones will turn to fish.

And if the bowl breaks
the water will fill the valleys,
make rivers of streams,
make lakes of waterfalls,
put roots in the sky
and branches in the sea,
like dust on the roof of time.
There were tolmec totem heads
and pyramids
and African cotton that was found
in the pre-Columbian Caribbean
which must've travelled by sea.
Whether aborigine or asiatic black
these islands were travelled on
many years before the fifth century.
And in that once upon
when the world was flat,
everyone could see each other,
so there were no secrets.
And anything set sail
from the Gambian coast
or from the Senegalese
was bound to drift to the Americas,
        eventually.

They knew that if you threw a stone
from Sierra Leone
it would bloom into islands, they knew the sea.
So they travelled by reed to reach
the Haitian coast
seeking the gold in the rivers and the nicotine.
There is evidence to suggest
that they were searching for that paradise
of the west, in the times of Rameses.
Because we find their footprints in Haiti,
in Jamaica, we find words of their tongues.
We find their breast bones in Trinidad,
bone dry fetish in rainforests,
and fragments of spaceships in Peru.
And many years later in 1492,
Columbus set sail for Japan
but instead he
found the caciques of the Bahamas
sitting in a cipher smoking pipes.
1502, there came ships from a distance
to a landfall in Mexico.
Precious cargo.
What would you carry
but your divinities and cosmology?
In Ifa there are similarities.
The zemi of the Taino for instance
were like those loas of turtles and snakes.
The Arawak also had spirits
which took on human shapes
like the great gods of Guinea;
distorted faces, mythical creatures
with elbows on the knees.

This is our lineage: the sea holds us here,
saves us from falling
off the side of the earth.
The more we change,
the more we stay the same.
'We spew ourselves up, but already,
underneath laughter can be heard.'[1]
The struggle continues
to define a space
to make this place our home.
While the diaspora unravels
like a broken necklace.

---

1 From Frantz Fanon, *Wretched of the Earth*

Girl with a Grenade

From Time *(2013)*

for Malala Yousafzai

The old man and his regime, east of nowhere,
kept a brace of hostages wrapt around him
      like a choir
And when they broke free to run he shot them
in the blazing sun.
But a girl escaped and ran
from their rickety aim.
She ran through the tall grass
      till she was
           ten miles hence.
I saw this close and hard and tactical
through lens riveted with ridges of death.
She hid amongst the turpentine trees,
beyond the ocean and the city.
Panorama of the infinite.
She was there.
Supernatural among the ramparts.
Carrying death
      in her palms.

It takes a child
to build such fire in the sky
to light a flame, it takes a heart,
a lung, a breath to carve a human space
— blood of madness,

for the sake of some abstract space
in your mind,
you would kill the child
burn down her home
then blow deep against all resistance.
You shot them down and put their bodies
in the ground
but here comes a girl
that won't be denied
carrying the truth
in trembling hands.

Heir (For Woman Who Wish)

From Time *(2013)*

she wished that her menopause would pass
then wished that I would grow tall
tall enough to step through the flood
then she wished upon the sun
that the old man wouldn't pull his gun on me
then she wished that I wouldn't swing my hand
or catch a spirit and fetch a blade, and run upon him
with broken bottles and rusty chains
she wished that I would move
to the cold part of the world
and when I got my chance she said take it
she didn't rock back on that dream
all the while she was making plans for me

she wished that the pain in her body would pass
she wished that the stain would fade
wished the diagnosis wrong and the prognosis bright
she wished that she could see another summer in London
wished that her hair would grow again
that I would love her like a first born son
that her body was just a cage that she could
step out of, catch a train up, catch a ride out
get back home to the hills
she wished upon these things and more
then she wished that I had daughters
and then she turned away
wished me safety on my night flight

while she watched the smoke fill the midday sky
she did not just pour sorrow on those dreams
she was busy making plans for me

wishes of women and women who wish
blood of my blood and flesh of my flesh

she wishes I could visit her down in the valley
where the calabash trees and our cousins roam
but my car got stuck down once
and strained its way back up
shows me her house, linoleum on the floor
shows me her kitchen, darkness
out from mountainsides, wishes I remember
how she bought me my first 45
and took me to the movies, like a father would
wishes I would call, that I would send my love
but I forget each time and think it's money she wants
she wishes the sky were higher
the rock poor dirt of this village life a bit lighter
but she don't rock back on that dream
all the while she was making plans for me

Shine

From Time *(2013)*

Like those Sundays in the country,
be that quality of light,
warm when it falls on the fields,
may you continue to shine.
Like light reveals
spells and blossoms on the trees,
be like sunshine
when it rains may you continue to dream.
We were running,
seemed no matter how fast
we were always running out of time.
And now I've been
in this foreign place
longer than I knew my own.
Am I still travelling
or am I finally home?
shine... shine...
We met in East Berlin.
The Jewish Hospital had let her out for a few hours,
But it was Sunday
snow was on the ground
and there was no place for us.
So we sat in a cafe
in the Turkish part of town
and we drank mint tea
while she did her best Chekhov.
But she'd lost herself so far inside the part

that I couldn't tell when she'd stopped acting.
She said, she can't cry in public
or show her arms because of the scars.
She wants to be loved
but she's angry all the time.
She is a seagull, with a broken wing.
She is an actress, with a trembling heart.
I watched her walk away into the cold cold night.
How could I tell her
that she's a star burning bright,
that she's beautiful
when she smiles?

Throw down your armies of despair.
Throw down your fear.
Throw down your pain.
You can learn to love the darkness
but let your light shine.
Like those Sundays in the country
be that quality of light.
Warm when it falls on the fields,
may you continue to shine.
Like light reveals
spells and blossoms on the trees
be like sunshine when it rains,
may you continue to dream.
Shine on, shine on

Kezi

From Time *(2013)*

Kezi is a woman have 9 children
An' she 7 months pregnant with twins

police come in, they knock down the door
while Kezi did gone to bathe

and they find 5 children aged 6 months to 8
in a wood shack that dilapidated

And they charge poor Kezi with abandonment
and give her six months in jail

and the people say, your honour have mercy please
the woman have 9 mouth to feed

but the people have no power unless they burn down a church
and seize the power that they need

and it have some who say that Kezi did bound
to go down in the Royal jail

how you will have nine children
and still want to make two more?

when you poor no arse and you cyar feed them
what you making baby for?

You eh see how water passing
where you squatting by the wharf, my lord

when rain fall is mud and jackass rat
that eating out your baby mouth

but you sit down on the courthouse steps and you cry
and you holding your head in your hand

well, if was me a give you six months more
and a take them children away

but the people have no power, so they plead and moan
but the judge won't throw out the case

Hear this one.

Ms Hady and her two daughters one Sunday
they walking, they coming from the the market

and a big van jump and cut them right down
only blood like marrow in the ground

and the people call out for justice
and they shut down the government road

cause the people have a right to break down the cage
if they voices will not be heard

then murder in the hills up above the city
gun pop, look a youthman dead

a stray bullet pass and enter one house
and shoot Mother Mavis dead

Now, Mavis was a woman that mind children
she feed them, she give them a home

so the people cry out for gun control
but cocaine doh have no soul

and the government still playing ego tricks
and they want resistance to dead

but we know guns are the teeth of democracy
so we aiming at politician head

is so things does go in a money city
when some people can't touch the gold

but even shanty town have cable tv
and the police making patrol

but some police corrupt, they kidnap and steal
they really don't give one fuck

but the people have the power to burn down the town
but they don't know the power that they got
      so, they get
         ——— *drag*

Suffering (This Savage Work)

From People of the Sun *(2018)*

You think a little bit a' suffer she suffer?
You think a little bit a' pressure she under?
  Is plenty!
You think a little bit a' pressure Tanty under?
Is not a little bit of hunger she suffer —
  is plenty!
Well, Tanty bound to suffer.
is like she bound to suffer
She have no land, no lumber.
Is only cockroach and thunder.
Then picture this picture:
is only cess pit or river,
is either duck bone or dog rice,
she give she life to sacrifice,
and every mouth want feeding
and Tanty sit down veranda,
she see the village how it changing,
she never touch computer.

Old dirt, nasty dirt,
worthless dirt, earthless hurt,
plenty dirt, bogus dirt,
dirt remaining since 1970.
Since Auntie dream of secretarial work
get put on hold for matrimony.
As if that were the pinnacle.
As if air-condition office
and shorthand proficiency
could beat back poverty

in that colony.
Either that, either that
or escape to New York —
skyscrape colony,
you make tall money,
you work three job and you weary
but eventually, you end up
right back up on that hill
with your kin and family.
Is perpetual slavery
in this colony.
When you born in poverty
your house does fall down easily.

Tanty, raise your hand but your hand can't raise.
That palm crimp and can't raise to groom it
— so cut it.
Speak your tongue but your tongue can't use.
Is only wind the throat pumping — pumping.
Beat your heart but the drum skin slack.
A-A, is only a Malta Carib the woman drink.
So in the middle of the dance
they had to stop the music —
and call for the ambulance.
And when the mark bus'
was a blood vessel burst
in Auntie good head.

Listen to the river but the river can't run.
Somebody say, 'The river dry, but is still a river.'
Yes, an' is years now Tanty waiting
to open she mouth —
to sing.

On the Move

From People of the Sun *(2018)*

after Liane Strauss

It was raining
      like a verb
like bone
      it was July
hard road
      maybe Marseille
up the mountain
      acrobatic
it was skin
      it was hid
back home
      it was written
Port of Spain
      we walked along
heavy light
      copacetic
heavy rain
      what was that
that was thunder
      wind that blew us
out of sync
      scenic time
it was odd
      a kind of shrimp
Caribbean

it was pulled back
to reveal it
　　　　it was London
we were sailing
　　　　we kept on it
it was midnight
　　　　we were moving
purple river
　　　　insect bone
it was a lie
　　　　no it wasn't
it was the truth
　　　　maybe more like
a long con
　　　　like love
as an anchor
　　　　pulls us under
it was repeated
　　　　like a chant
like a hymn
　　　　like a dirge
like a bell
　　　　it was gravel
rugged pitch
　　　　a blow that left a
wound in water
　　　　wild fever
fever grass
　　　　it was patchouli
orange blossom
　　　　it was something
like madness

            it was painted
with desire
            baptist heat
so elastic
            glossolalia
spirit talking

Once when freedom had meaning
like organs of heat in the evening
my body held vibrations of the Caribbean
and we let bled that excess negritude of being
but the past didn't last long
it grew tired and we wept in forests
where black myth was painted
in that acrobatic silence
and now my soul still holds
the aroma of anguish

do not gaze
            not too long
upon the past
            its so dissonant
bass notes
            sky church
steady dying
            we were waiting
to burst out of
            human life
into brightness
            heading east
to the ocean
            too shallow

to drown in
        rugged steep
we were coming
        back from drowning
Manzanilla
        old plantation
history was
        all around us
it was fluid
        rhythm motion
on the move

So shallow is this memory
that it pierced me like
Chiricahuan arrowhead
drowned it in: double beaten goatskin
drums from gust and plywood junctions
— bliss throat sparkles there
like sea silt in jetty fish
near Port Authority where
cruise ships landed to this dreamscape
contemplating the road
Our verge of memory
split with cane like canboulay
in a place where
everything happens at once

Calling England Home

From The Rich Are Only Defeated
When Running for Their Lives *(2021)*

Black and been here since 1949
— West London jaw grind, 'Tek it easy.'
We saw him, you saw him
walking along the canal last night.
And what a joy to buck up upon him
at the carnival today,
to hear him speak about
the dances and the bands
at the Paramount,
the spots you couldn't mix
with white in, or dance in.
Remembering...London.

> How he been slapped so hard
> with the lash — Sam Selvon say.
> And it take him 60 years
> before he could call England
> 'home.'

He musta come here in black and white.
1959, time longer than twine.
So long ago he don't remember being a child,
Just a suit and steamer trunk
upon a ship which took a good six weeks to cross.
We sat at his kitchen table
and I filmed him on the sly
but he wasn't saying much

at least nothing I could put in a poem,
instead he showed me
photographs — with the dashiki and the fez
with Michael X at The Ambience.

      Outside the night came in,
      and he had moved so far away
      from calling England
      'home'.

I've lived here longer than home, since 1989.
Remember Harlesden in the spring time.
I used to walk from Cricklewood
to Marylebone High Street
to cut up meat to punch out dough
I was never asked to wait tables
or to serve scones and coffee.
I worked in the basement.
But I soon learned to tie my apron
in a way that retained some dignity.

      And in my first summer above the corner shop,
      I listened to rare groove on pirate radio.
      I was flung so far from any notion of nation.
      How long do you have to live in a place
      before you can call it
      'home'?

Language

From The Rich Are Only Defeated
When Running For Their Lives *(2021)*

> To name something is to wait for it
> in a place where you think it will pass.
> — AMIRI BARAKA

Something about how we have names for everything.
How each leaf has its place at the shaded side of the river,
the dark dirt under the cocoa onion, has a name
for that kind of soil. The soft
      cup of scales
forming the echeveria
      has a name,
the way it folds. The filament
in the light of the firefly — the wick, the tail
has a name —
      luciferin, in the production of light.
Water in the knee and it has a name
— meniscus — effusion
which is really, a form of
      liquid textology —
      dividing the meat into chunk and gill.

      Once
there were still unseen places and things,
corners of experience which had no name,
and so you could walk upon them
and meet them solid for the first time

be dubwise and dread and hail them up
and bump locks head.
      Dread.
And my grandmother said
that if the flying frog leapt
and landed on your face, or the soft
fold of your arm,
that it would stay there,
attach itself
as if with glue
and you would have to
iron or steam steel, impress
upon the frog-back skin till it stick to the stainless heat,
until it release
      an' peel off.

We returned from country visits, from visiting kin or churches
hid in bush to find: flying frogs: perched in corners of the house.
Trapped in their silence of peace, I never saw their leap.
But I seen what hurricanes could do to islands.
I seen it on TV and it had a name.

    Nigropalmatus
    Hylidae
    Rhacophorus
        — fringe-limbed or marvellous
    Ecnomiohyla
    Polypedates

       — in the calabash tree
       — where it has a name.

My cousin Alvin and the hillside
where bananas are grown from seed.
This place has a dance, and it has a name,
Even vinegar has a seed.
We were wild
         children.
We had names with which we
moved through space
                    like blades.

Smallholding: Eclogue

From Caribbean Roots *(2016)*

We never went hungry,
we never suffered destitution.
That was never our history.
Our history was of revolution.

That is why my grandfather persisted with his toil
to root dasheen and cassava, to peel the great ear of its leaf.
The sea green banana with its temporal trunk was to be cut
and flung to the mud, and although there was no
discernible scheme, at least not to us, perhaps the old man
was compelled to plant those trees along routes
embedded in the maps of his palms,
because history had tied him to the land
and he could never break free.

This acre was his heritage,
he knew each bean crop or ripple of bees,
the purple sugar of the cane, planted not for sugar
but because it had always been.
The parakeets, the river near, that little house
which nevertheless sage or gully burst
withstood hurricanes and blows.
The frizzle neck hen and the man cock to kill,
the drake that caws — bucolic in this eclogue.

So that even in suburbs, far from mountain towns or farms
he would still cultivate a homestead, an orchid,

he would irrigate a small ravine.
Spit down from the wash mouth sink
in the cold water room, the soil, its yield, his hands, blending
into the sweet mud of his sweat.

One day the sun might be shining,
the rain might be falling, same time,
the devil and his wife might be fighting for a hambone,
and that bush was broad, remember, the veritable gust
of light, a vision: a view of hills and herbs.
And besides, Miss Henry was in her veranda
shelling peas and watching.

And at some point the seed pod buds
and bursts through the limit of air.
This is what we had, and we worked with it.
We were given a small holding, we were thrown the husk,
but there was something in the way the sunlight splashed
against the side of the house on Sunday afternoon
—there was something
        in that light.

Drum Song

From Caribbean Roots *(2016)*

for Richie Havens

sometimes he was so overwhelmed
by the percussive power of his own soul
that he hid in the shut-eye song
      concentration deep
in a dark well of hours
sweat moving on the waters
towards some apex of umbilical light
where he became a mood
           a vibration
the resonance of wood
a man made of earth
a man made of dirt and oil and eyes
and hands that spanned
            frets and wings of flying things
         densities in ten cities emerging
into cubic space
    but what is a drum
        a drum is a moon
            a drum is a heel
                a drum is a heel a heel
                    a drum is a heel a drum is a fist
    beating
    a drum is the earth
        and what is the earth
            the sound of a drum

the sound of our souls colliding

his joy was as hard as time
painful to earn transcendent in tears and years
he had come in beads and robes
he had walked across the desert from the niger bend
but then he fell off his stool and lost himself in the song
hard to mend, the river bend.
he had been singing of the zodiac — he had been
strumming his steel strung drum — he had been
ringing the bell of his heart

he was made of earth and wood and stone and branches and
    bone and field
hollers and moans and sea shanties pulling — *reel man holler*
                                        reel and pull
                                        reel man holler
                                        reel and pull

he was a man among men and when he shook your hand
you knew that he had penetrated deep into the mangrove
with large hands   the swamplands
he had gone deep into some wild island jungle
        stay with us we cried but he was always here
        stay with us but we were the ones
                    who were leaving
and he sat on the old stump of a cedar tree rooted in the dark dirt
muted by the blues and sadness of the world
sometimes he played sad songs
but he could make them sound
so beautiful
so beautiful

that even hummingbirds may rest for a while
in the palms of his hands

he wears black
he wears silver rings on each finger
and when he sings the clouds would move with his breath
exhale
to the litmus of magic
to the frequency of magic
to the tumble down like cathedrals falling
feet beating the earth to freedom
he lay deep in the groove
so far back that we forgot he was there
and we went on grinning and grinding and shucking and jiving
against sweaty walls in european halls forgetting that we were
drummers
forgetting that we were black
forgetting that in fact that we were naked
that we were deeper than shadows
steep like wire transmits the elliptical
be dense with fury be dynamic be fierce be devious
be brazen be wailing in the weeping
sometimes he sang so deep that he didn't even know
that he was standing on the bottom of the sea reaching up
to catch us from falling

what is a drum
a drum is a drum a drum is a heel
duke said a drum is a woman
a drum is the pulse of sex and oil and heat
a drum is the skin a drum is alive
a drum is to play but not to beat
or to be beaten

the funk between the meat
to sweeten the heat
a drum is a drummer
be the drum
be the rhythm
be the drum.

> *reel man holler*
> *reel and pull*
> *reel man holler*
> *reel and pull*

Brother Davis (Yanvalou)

From Caribbean Roots *(2016)*

Brother Davis was building a Trojan horse of straw
in a deep river for the king. And the river was snarling
and rising, and the waters came upon him
but he worked on, he put his back against the waves.
He tied the nape, the strands of mane,
he built the back, he grooved and planed,
he built the bones of its head.
He put hooks and eyes and cupid hairpins
and then he crowned it with gold.
But the river took the crown and sailed it away
when Brother Davis wasn't looking.
And I shouted from a high place, I said, 'Oh, Brother Davis,
looks like the river done stole your crown.'
And Brother Davis swam fast as he could
through the waters, like a gospel plough,
but he just could not reach it.
He swam past the saw mill and the ice factory,
past the religious prison and the poor house.
Might be zangee eel in that water — whip snake,
might be your church is burning down.
Oh, Brother Davis, now your Trojan Horse is sinking down.
Looks like your church is, like your church is burning down.
And the crowd that searches from the river bank
with their infinite mercy
they couldn't save Brother Davis,
and the water turned to brown.

Caribbean Roots

From Caribbean Roots *(2016)*

Our history is not colonialism and slavery.
Our history is our struggle against
enslavement and colonialism.
— EARL LOVELACE

Look how long we out here
and we still looking somewhere else for roots.
When your great-great grandfather rooted in the earth,
and your great-great grandmother live to be 102.
That not root? That not root enough for you?
When we born and grow in these islands
and learn to fly from cliff top to tree top and never find
what we looking for in no metropolitan or old colonial planet.
So come on, dip yourself in the salt,
set yourself like roots
      Caribbean roots.

      Bahama roots,
      Barbadian roots,
      Grenadian roots,
      Puerto Rican roots,
      Jamaican roots,
      where you born, where you born you root,
      Caribbean roots!
      Set yourself in the soil,
      put your head in the sky,

Caribbean roots!
Where you born, where you born you root.

You may find yourself
sitting in a plane on a runway in Berlin.
You may find yourself in Brittany, or Paris or Rome.
You might find yourself in Barcelona,
or Oxford or Copenhagen.
And suddenly you realise,
you say, 'But wait, I aint European.'
You realise that you're rooted in the muck of some history
and you begin to look around at the majesty
of old Europe, at the citadels of its power
at its grand architecture, set in old stone,
you begin to ask yourself, 'Where are my monuments?
How come all these monuments, even the ones in the islands,
were built by those who colonised and enslaved me?'
You need to set your self in the roots,
Caribbean roots.
Set yourself in the soil
of these Caribbean roots.

My friend come from Guadeloupe,
he say, 'Mister, don't call me French.'
He say, 'France like to make everything French
but not me, y'see, don't forget that we are
Caribbean people.
Brother man, we all suffer in the same breeze
to be torn from the heat,
and even now, we're still in the midst of the battle.
We are the roots, Caribbean roots.'

Trinidad is roots,
Tobago roots,
Martiniquan roots,
Guadeloupe is roots,
Montserrat is roots,
Virgin Island roots,
St Vincent roots,
where you born you root,
Caribbean roots.
Dip yourself in the salt,
put your head in the sky!
Caribbean roots...Caribbean Roots
where you born, where you born you root...

Cobra

From Rubber Orchestras *(2011)*

As he leapt the wild road
All I could do was whisper his name
Cobra...cobra
invincible
irrepressible
incredibly strong
But where he was he was
I thought he might have
left south-east and gone north
I thought he might have —
I hadn't seen the mighty cobra
for two years long
not since the Afrofuturist party at the art gallery
I hadn't seen him
in the rugged record shop where I was working
with perspiration pooling in his pockets
listening to Joe Gibbs 12s and Defunkt
with headphones
Cobra
leaping like a snake
his long limbs swinging like whips
gold satin shirt
with the billowing
black star on the back
with the billowing
trousers tapered at the ankle
slick as a snake's shadow

taller leaner and strange
with his head held up
as he leapt over cars and enemies
and all I could do was whisper his name
softly after and into the rush of the wind he pulls —
C o b r a...cobra
softly after and into the rush of the wind he pulls —
C o b r a...cobra
and all I could do was whisper his name
as he leapt over cars and enemies
with his head held up
taller leaner and strange
slick as a snake's shadow
trousers tapered at the ankle
with the billowing
black star on the back
with the billowing
gold satin shirt
his long limbs swinging like whips
leaping like a snake
Cobra
with headphones
listening to Joe Gibbs 12 and Defunkt
in the rugged record shop where I was working
with perspiration pooling in his pockets
not since the Afrofuturist party at the art gallery
I hadn't seen him
for two years long
I hadn't seen the mighty cobra
I thought he might have —
left south-east and gone north
I thought he might have

But where he was he was
incredibly strong
irrepressible
invincible
All I could do was whisper his name
Cobra...cobra
As he leapt the wild road

Acknowledgments

The three decades of writing collected here deserves a vast list of gratitudes. I have forgotten a few names along the way, so what follows is incomplete and still evolving.

Love x Love to my support system, my tribe of powerful women – Louise, Keiko & Meena.

To my brother Dennis, to my sisters, and my family in Trinidad and the UK.

To Bruce Barnes, Frances Presley and Brian Doherty from the Islington Poetry Workshop – circa 1993/1994 – where I first learned the value of being part of a community of poets, and where my work was nurtured by their generosity of spirit and supportive critique.

To Lauri Scheyer, for her love and support for the last two decades, for teaching me that the personal is the universal, and for always being a beacon of guidance and pure energy.

To my dirt heart UK foundation poetry community: Roger Robinson, Malika Booker, Nick Makoha, Francesca Beard, Inua Ellams, Nii Parkes, Karen McCarthy Woolf, Patience Agbabi, Jacob Sam-La Rose.

To my beloved and trusted editor Kayo Chingonyi. Thank you Kayo, for the strength of your vision, for the things you say and the spaces in-between.

To the team at Bloomsbury for their patience and dedication to magic.

To my cherished agent Elise Dillsworth for 15 years of dedication and support, from the root to the blossom.

To James Oscar Jr. for science and secret technology, for Joans, Artaud, Glissant, Breton.

To Nancy Hospedales, Bernadine Phillip and the ladies of Policy Service/Tatil Life (circa 1986–89) who knew I was writing poems when I should have been working.

To Chris & Jen Hamilton Emery/Salt, to Melanie Abrahams/Renaissance One, to Nathalie Teitler, Blake Morrison, Maura Dooley, to Sharmilla Beezmohun and Speaking Volumes, OCM Bocas Lit Fest and New Beacon Books. To Linton Kwesi Johnson, Tom Chivers, Vanessa Richards, Khefri Riley, Kelly Josephs, Jason Yarde, Peter Kahn, Naomi Woddis, Silvia Gasparo Moro, Monique Roffey, Franck Descollonges, Antoine Rajon, Sascha Akhtar, Nathaniel Mackey, Keziah Jones and Earl Lovelace.

To Allison Barry and Nia Roberts who typeset my first two collections, to Adrian Owusu for the artwork in *Desafinado*, and as always, to Martin La Borde & Roderick Chasseau.

I also offer gratitudes to the numerous musicians who have lent their art to uplift some of these poems into solid life. But mostly to Colin Webster and Andrew John for decades of friendship and ring craft, for whispering the words to my poems when I forget them on stage.

I am grateful too, to the following journals and anthologies in which some of these poems first appeared: *Red: Contemporary Black British Poetry, Black Brown & Beige: Surrealist Writings from Africa and the Diaspora, Identity Crisis – New British and Irish Poets, Out of Bounds: British Black & Asian Poets, More Fiya, The Golden Shovel Anthology, Long Poem* magazine, *Caribbean Review of Books, Wasafari, Poetry Salzburg Review, Statement* magazine, *Prairie Schooner.*

A Note on the Author

Anthony Joseph is a poet, novelist, academic and musician whose work explores the transnational vibrations of the African Diaspora. The author of five poetry collections, three novels and nine critically acclaimed albums, Joseph's work has explored the aesthetics of Caribbean Poetry among other subjects. *Sonnets for Albert* was awarded the 2022 T. S. Eliot Prize and the OCM Bocas Prize for Poetry in 2023, and was shortlisted for the Forward Prize for Poetry. He is a Fellow of the Royal Society of Literature and a Lecturer in Creative Writing at King's College, London.

A Note on the Type

Warnock is a serif typeface designed by Robert Slimbach. The design features sharp, wedge-shaped serifs. The typeface is named after John Warnock, one of the co-founders of Adobe. John Warnock's son, Chris Warnock, requested that Slimbach design the typeface as a tribute to his father in 1997. It was later released as a commercial font by Adobe in 2000 under the name Warnock Pro.